THE RIVER'S VOICE

THE RIVER'S VOICE

VOICE

An Anthology of Poetry

edited by Angela King and Susan Clifford for
Common Ground

Green Books

First published in 2000
by Green Books Ltd
Foxhole, Dartington
Totnes, Devon TQ9 6EB

in association with Common Ground
P.O. Box 25309, London NW5 1ZA

Cover design by Rick Lawrence
Cover illustration © Clifford Harper 1999

Text printed by Biddles Ltd, Guildford, Surrey
on Five Seasons 100% recycled paper

British Library Cataloguing in Publication Data
The River's Voice: an anthology of poetry

I. Poetry in English. Special subjects. Rivers. Anthologies
I. King, Angela, II. Clifford, Susan

ISBN 1 870098 82 X

Contents

Preface

The River Meander must be a wonderful sight, its Turkish curves so tantalising that it has given the English language a verb and a noun. King Tantalos, up to his neck in Phrygian water that receded whenever he bent his head to drink, gave us the teasing verb. Intricate language and stories hang in the air, condensing when needed to enrich another place. Springs and great rivers—and all those bournes, becks, burns and brooks in between—not only provide us with our basic requirement for life, but have helped us to explain and to share knowledge of the world around us.

The real rivers, which may terrorise or delight us, are intriguing for their particularity. The variegation found in a single river valley and the differences among catchments are part of the great workings of nature, time and geology, and the efforts that we humans have made to control and use water for our own ends.

Even in England, where we had learnt to share the power of the stream with wild creatures and plants, leating it to drive mills, diverting it to flood meadows, damming it to pacify and to please, some of our activities are having profound implications. Through two centuries of industrialisation, we have turned our back on the city river; in only five decades, intensifying farming practices have filled the country river with chemicals; engineering has straightened the meanders, rendering the river more, not less, unpredictable. Fashions in fear, and development, have conspired to push running water away from our everyday experience, increasingly reducing streams to ditches and finally to culverts. The explosion in the working and domestic use of water is depleting aquifers, those banks of ancient water, and causing the drying up of streams. And the selling of common water into corporate hands is surely the retreat of the millennium.

We are united in our need for water, but are increasingly divided by its scarcity, its profusion—or big ideas for its use.

Think of Aral, the biggest lake in central Asia, which is now dry, and of the huge dams along the Hwang Ho; contemplate the impact of shrinking polar ice caps and retreating glaciers in the Rockies and Himalayas. Then look at the spring, stream or river that is the reason why your settlement is where it is.

At the very moment when we need the closeness of water to feed our humanity and imagination, we seem to be denied literal contact, and have lost sight and sound of its magic.

Our aspiration in bringing together mainly twentieth-century poetry in this anthology is to demonstrate a richness—seen and heard by keen observers with the capacity to distil ideas, language, and stories—which continues to offer a route to our own imaginations.

What the poems also show is our willingness to be inspired by the particularity of actual rivers. One simple observation links ancient wisdoms with fractal science, aesthetic observation with the seepage of language and names: 'All rivers, small or large, agree in one character, they like to lean a little on one side.' (John Ruskin, *The Elements of Drawing*, 1857.) Common Ground's work is based upon an idea of getting there better in the long run by going the long way round.

Susan Clifford and Angela King
Common Ground
October 1999

Foreword

I know of few people and no poet for whom water is not a first love. We all spend the first eternal dreamtime of our lives in the same internal mother ocean, so even after we have lost our gills and dived into the world, we are forever water babies, responding playfully to the least drenching; singing in the rain or in the bath, thinking or dreaming wild thoughts as we are borne weightless in the swimming pool, the river or the sea. D. H. Lawrence had the idea that you could tell the true water-people, like Herman Melville, by their blue eyes, and that 'we are most of us who use the English language water-people, sea-derived.' W. H. Auden thought all poetry should sound like running water, and his line 'A culture is no better than its woods' would ring just as true for rivers.

The realisation that rivers and woods are the measure of our civilisation is no different from the notion that you can tell a man by his shoes. It was brought home to me a year or two ago as I lay beside a limestone pool in the Gordale Beck in a sunny cleft above the famous Gordale Scar waterfall in the Yorkshire Dales near Malham. It was a hot day; all the hotter after a scramble up the tufa steps beside the cascade, and I had been bathing in the crystalline water. I imagined how this merry, jingling beck would soon become a river, the Aire, then flow on through Skipton and Leeds and eventually join other rivers in the turbid tide of the Humber, shedding its innocence all the way, reflecting the state of the land and air around it. Writing about water, and its modern suppression through technology and engineering, Adam Nicolson recently remarked how 'it has come to look like the subconscious of the landscape, a vehicle for its dreams and a sump for its poisons.' It seems science can fix almost anything these days, except the Humber.

You cannot go near a river, or any water, without thinking of history. My own favourite stretch is still the slow river of the moat across the lawn behind my house in Suffolk, and when I gaze into its reflected clouds and trees with the filmy world of newts and water weed moving about beneath like a double exposure, it feels 'deep as England'. It must have been dug by hand at enormous expenditure of labour and, probably, pain as well, someone having divined the spring in its depths that keeps it clear and invisibly flowing. To prefer one's own, most intimately known Walden Pond might seem narcissistic, and in gazing into the mirror of water, it is true that we stare into our own souls. We are ourselves nine-tenths water, have feelings that overflow or brim over, and writers, especially, dread drying up.

All poets are diviners, dowsing for the 'Third Thing', as D. H. Lawrence calls it, that comes about when you juxtapose unlikely atoms like hydrogen and oxygen and the whole sparks into more than the sum of its parts, 'the divine pen twisting in the hand', as Dannie Abse says. In the beginning, the divine was water, and to dowse it was an act of faith. The French verb *deviner* can mean guessing at anything, from a riddle to a source. The original divines, or diviners, simply intuited the presence of god, which in those days was water, and as far as U. A. Fanthorpe is concerned (see 'Water Everywhere'), still is. Philip Larkin seems to have agreed, when he wrote that if he were called in to construct a religion he would make use of water.

Water is the most poetical of elements, allowing of no sudden, awkward movements: even a stone dropped in sinks gracefully. No element ranges in form so dramatically from ice to invisible vapour. Even in the midst of turbulent chaos, water conforms strictly to the laws of mathematics, as a poem holds to its metre or form. One of the great sea swimmers of our age, Sir James Lighthill, sometime Lucasian Professor of Mathematics at Cambridge, proved this when he correctly calculated how to harness the notorious tidal currents that tear around the Channel Island of Sark and circumnavigated the island on six separate occasions.

The history of a river is often most apparent in its natural history: in the timeless running of the salmon or eels, the arrival of sand-martins from far across the sea to nest in a bank, or in the march of toads along an ancient route to spawn. The wild creatures and their ritual journeys are as unstoppable and rhythmical as the river itself, unless we interfere, in the blind way we so often do—as in the case of the mayflies on the River Test at Stockbridge, who, in the Spring of 1920, laid their eggs on the glistening surface of the newly tarred village street after a rainstorm.

Mutability is also evident in all the forms of things in the river, which always wants to round everything to its own patterns of flow and is forever in a state of flux itself: 'Nobody steps into the same river twice,' says Derek Mahon, quoting Heraclitus. Where others might meditate on their mortality with the help of a skull, my desk is cluttered with stones and sticks from rivers I have explored and swum all over the country. A tiny megalith of striated mauve sandstone came out of the bed of the Usk near Talybont at a sandy bend in the river, its corners and edges well on the way to being rounded into a sphere. About two inches cubed, it caught my eye in one of those beaver-jams of sticks and stones and bits of torn plastic that accumulate as river flotsam at the still centre of a beached vortex. The eddy curls upon itself like a question mark and leaves this full stop.

The action of the water has much the same effect on bits of wood as on the stone. Amongst my relics from the Usk, which seems a specially magical river to me, is a duck's beak of hazel and a tiny boomerang of ash so bleached it could be bone, where only the tough knot of an elbow has survived the river's sandpapering. Every tree is a stream of sap. How much of a tree is ebbing and flowing you discover when you saw up logs and dry them out in a stack for a year or two. The seasoned wood is so much lighter than the sapwood. On a summer's day thousands of gallons are drawn through an acre of woodland to evaporate through the leaves into the atmosphere. And when a river runs into the sea at low tide it pencils the form of a tree on the wet sand. Conversely, my wooden relics are full of the same eddies and whorls as the river's own body. Little swirling knotholes like whirlpools, and the undulating flow of grain.

If you made a very slow-motion stop-frame aerial film of a river's restless history, it would look like a swimming snake. In the fens, rivers are forever changing course, building up banks of silt which eventually burst, releasing the river to set off on a new course across country to the sea, leaving only the roddon: the dry bed. At Welney, you can walk along the deserted roddon of the Cam, and the River Wissey no longer flows anywhere near Wisbech, to which it gave a name. People often talk about rivers following the contours of the land, but it is quite the other way about. It is the land that follows the rivers and streams, and the glaciers before them. That is another way a river is a god, as the creator of our landscape, shaping it, feeding it, sometimes drowning it. When T. S. Eliot calls a river 'a strong brown god' in 'The Dry Salvages', he goes on to say that it is a 'reminder/ Of what men choose to forget.' Perhaps this book, too, is a reminder of things we have half-forgotten, a collective quest for the nymphs Eliot says have departed and left no addresses; for that elusive 'Third Thing'.

Out walking on the Black Hill near the river Wye recently after a week of heavy rains, springs were rising out of the hillside all round me with such urgency they were lifting turf, and with such hydraulic power they would not be stopped if I stepped on them. A poem can exert hydraulic power, and with the same subtlety. Like a river and like love, it 'begins in delight and ends in wisdom'. Robert Frost, who lived in snowy New Hampshire, put it this way: 'Like a piece of ice on a hot stove, the poem must ride on its own melting.'

Roger Deakin
September 1999

Dear water, clear water, playful in all your streams

W. H. Auden

'Above all rivers thy river hath renown'

Above all rivers thy river hath renown,
Whose beryl streamès, pleasant and preclare,
Under thy lusty wallès runneth down;
Where many a swan doth swim with wingès fair,
Where many a barge doth sail, and row with oar,
Where many a ship doth rest with top-royal.
O town of townès, patron and not compare,
London, thou art the flower of Cities all.

William Dunbar
from 'To the City of London'

Abstracted Water

Abstracted water, captive for a while,
becomes abstract, a proposition in hydraulics,

slops through lock-machines, goes level,
carries coal, parties, makes money,

slides back into Nature, used. If it hadn't come
leaking out of the hills to be cornered

you could synthesize it: a float-medium,
liquid vermiculite, a thin gel

flavoured with diesel,
rust, warm discharges.

The Cut's a notion, an idea cleaner than a river,
and closed at both ends. It's venture-water.

The design depth doesn't allow for motor-bikes, or
layers of sunken gondolas from supermarkets;

Garbage In, Garbage Out. The boat called 'Heritage'
comes dredging. Nothing much fronts

the canal. Where buildings on a street
stare you out, here it's you who do the looking,

left in your peace a little way
from the backside of it all, among

blank, patched-up walls with huge
secrets that stink and flare,

piss out coloured suds. Secrets
half-guarded, absorbed; secrets forgotten,

left to decay, bursting apart,
letting the dead stuff spill out. Sunlight

under bridges stays enclosed,
lattices to and fro. There's a law

dirt grows out of.

Roy Fisher

Along Almost Any River

It has converted to its own purposes
My loose sense of absence, twisting
With its vapid curvatures the mind's exclusion
Into awareness of declivities and the waterfowl.

For several hours, therefore, having neither strength
Nor a rival accuracy, I have walked
In reluctant indenture along the bank,
Exercising the faculties in the forms of compassion.

And why should I now, simply out of weakness,
Keep open house to the spurious decision
Of swans and their indifferent currents? To ask
Is not to refute, but a kind of knowledge;

That the struggle will be elsewhere, not fluent, but a locked
And stammering combat between divided geologies.
Here at the source it is the riven fault
That the water will spring from, floating the lucent swans.

J. H. Prynne

Anahorish

My 'place of clear water',
the first hill in the world
where springs washed into
the shiny grass

and darkened cobbles
in the bed of the lane.
Anahorish, soft gradient
of consonant, vowel-meadow,

after-image of lamps
swung through the yards
on winter evenings.
With pails and barrows

those mound-dwellers
go waist-deep in mist
to break the light ice
at wells and dunghills.

Seamus Heaney

Angler

His waders among the water-crowfoot,
intent behind his sunglasses, he casts repeatedly,
does not see me pass.
                              I sit
on the riverbank, see the meadowsweet,
agrimony, remembered dragonflies,
hear the water break the channel, cast about
for words.
                      Later
he trudges past, his creel
empty, sees my empty
notebook, smiles a secret smile
of complicity.

Adrian Henri
(Totleigh Barton, Devon)

At Dunkeswell Abbey

Below the ford, the stream in flood
Rises and laps the leaf-choked wood
And fallen branches trap thick mud.
Pebbles are swept like slingstones down
Runnels and channels sliced through stone
And in the hollows sink and drown.

On either side broad ramparts hold
The water back from copse and field,
Where a dry earthbank seems to fold
Protectively a hollow space
Of pasture edged with stunted trees
In its inert and curved embrace.

Six hundred years ago, great pike
Grown old in this man-fashioned lake
Swam through its lily clusters like
Dream-presences below the mind.
Dark waters stirred where now I stand
Hearing the distant stream unwind.

The stillness here was made to last.
Whatever shapes survive exist
In some faint diagram of the past,
A sketch-map tentative as those
Robbed walls whose simulacrum lies
In patches summer droughts expose.

One wall still overtops the trees
Beyond the ford, but bramble grows
Round rotten stone. What energies
Persist are harnessed to the stream,
Violent in flood, not curbed or tame,
And hurtling without plan or aim.

Anthony Thwaite

At the Sand Creek Bridge

The path of most insistence
Constrains the creek
Where it spools
And rummages through
Its darkest secrets
And the mooncolored trout revolve.
If it's been a long time coming
It'll be a long time gone.
Or so I think, watching it
Neither hurry nor tarry
Through spills and basins
I used to climb among

With a fly rod between my teeth,
And may again
If life is long.
Now I'm content to idle
The truck on the bridge
As the pines offer
Their shadows to water.
I can still remember
A few things.
The years I wasted fishing
Down here.
Cold rock under fingertips
And the smell of willow early.
The lapidary green
Of the little snake
Who swims like water in water.
The sun getting hotter
On my shoulders,
My feet in the current
Going numb.
Once I stood on the canyon rim
And hurled boulders
One after another down,
To boom and ricochet,
To make the shadows speak.
There was no one anywhere
To hear the canyon's utterance
Or how the quiet rushed back hard
When I stopped,
My loneliness complete,
The smell of gunpowder
In the air.

James Galvin

The Baite

Come live with mee, and bee my love,
And we will some new pleasures prove
Of golden sands, and christall brookes,
With silken lines, and silver hookes.

There will the river whispering runne
Warm'd by thy eyes, more then the Sunne.
And there th'inamor'd fish will stay,
Begging themselves they may betray.

When thou wilt swimme in that live bath,
Each fish, which every channell hath,
Will amorously to thee swimme,
Gladder to catch thee, then thou him.

If thou, to be so seene, beest loath,
By Sunne, or Moone, thou darknest both,
And if my selfe have leave to see,
I need not their light, having thee.

Let others freeze with angling reeds,
And cut their legges, with shells and weeds
Or treacherously poore fish beset,
With strangling snare, or windowie net:

Let coarse bold hands, from slimy nest
The bedded fish in banks out-wrest,
Or curious traitors, sleavesilke flies
Bewitch poore fishes wandring eyes.

For thee, thou needst no such deceit,
For thou thy selfe art thine owne bait;
That fish, that is not catch'd thereby,
Alas, is wiser farre then I.

John Donne

Ballade to a Fish of the Brooke

Why flyest thou away with fear?
Trust me, there's nought of danger near,
  I have no wicked hooke
All covered with a snaring bait,
Alas, to tempt thee to thy fate,
  And dragge thee from the brooke.

O harmless tenant of the flood,
I do not wish to spill thy blood,
  For Nature unto thee
Perchance hath given a tender wife,
And children dear, to charme thy life,
  As she hath done for me.

Enjoy thy streams, O harmless fish;
And when an angler, for his dish,
  Through gluttony's vile sin,
Attempts, a wretch, to pull thee *out*,
God give thee strength, O gentel trout,
  To pull the raskall *in*!

John Wolcot

The Banished Gods

Paros, far-shining star of dark-blue earth,
  Reverts to the sea its mother.
    The tiny particles,
  Rose quartz and amethyst,
Panic into the warm brine together.

Near the headwaters of the longest river
  There is a forest clearing,
    A dank, misty place
  Where light stands in columns
And birds sing with a noise like paper tearing.

Far from land, far from the trade routes,
  In an unbroken dream-time
    Of penguin and whale
  The seas sigh to themselves
Reliving the days before the days of sail.

Down a dark lane at the back of beyond
  A farm dog lies by a dead fire
    Dreaming of nothing
  While a window goes slowly grey
Brightening a laid table and hung clothing.

Where the wires end the moor seethes in silence,
  Scattered with scree, primroses,
    Feathers and faeces;
  It shelters the hawk and hears
In dreams the forlorn cries of lost species.

It is here that the banished gods are in hiding,
  Here they sit out the centuries
    In stone, water
  And the hearts of trees,
Lost in a reverie of their own natures—

Of zero-growth economics and seasonal change
  In a world without cars, computers
    Or nuclear skies,
  Where thought is a fondling of stones
And wisdom a five-minute silence at moonrise.

Derek Mahon

The Banks of Nith

I

The Thames flows proudly to the sea,
  Where royal cities stately stand;
But sweeter flows the Nith, to me,
  Where Cummins ance had high command:
When shall I see that honour'd land,
  That winding stream I love so dear!
Must wayward fortune's adverse hand
  For ever, ever keep me here?

II

How lovely, Nith, thy fruitful vales,
  Where spreading hawthorns gaily bloom!
How sweetly wind thy sloping dales,
  Where lambkins wanton thro' the broom!
Tho' wandering, now, must be my doom,
  Far from thy bonnie banks and braes,
May there my latest hours consume,
  Amang the friends of early days!

                                        Robert Burns

Bathing

Oh, many a time have I, a five years' child,
In a small mill-race severed from his stream,
Made one long bathing of a summer's day;
Basked in the sun, and plunged and basked again
Alternate, all a summer's day, or scoured
The sandy fields, leaping through flowery groves
Of yellow ragwort; or when rock and hill,
The woods, and distant Skiddaw's lofty height,
Were bronzed with deepest radiance, stood alone
Beneath the sky, as if I had been born

On Indian plains, and from my mother's hut
Had run abroad in wantonness, to sport,
A naked savage, in the thunder shower.

William Wordsworth

Beck

Not the beck only,
Not just the water—
The stones flow also,
Slow
As continental drift,
As the growth of coral,
As the climb
Of a stalagmite.
Motionless to the eye,
Wide cataracts of rock
Pour off the fellside,
Throw up a spume
Of gravel and scree
To eddy and sink
In the blink of a lifetime.
The water abrades,
Erodes; dissolves
Limestones and chlorides;
Organizes its haulage—
Every drop loaded
With a millionth of a milligramme of fell.
The falling water
Hangs steady as stone;
But the solid rock
Is a whirlpool of commotion,
As the fluid strata
Crest the curl of time,
And top-heavy boulders
Tip over headlong,

An inch in a thousand years.
A Niagara of chock-stones,
Bucketing from the crags,
Spouts down the gullies.
Slate and sandstone
Flake and deliquesce,
And in a grey
Alluvial sweat
Ingleborough and Helvellyn
Waste daily away.
The pith of the pikes
Oozes to the marshes,
Slides along the sykes,
Trickles through ditch and dub,
Enters the endless
Chain of water,
The pull of earth's centre—
An irresistible momentum,
Never to be reversed,
Never to be halted,
Till the tallest fell
Runs level with the lowland,
And scree lies flat as shingle,
And every valley is exalted,
Every mountain and hill
Flows slow.

Norman Nicholson

Behind the Waterfall

The waterfall is at its best today:
satisfyingly huge, it booms from its rock wall
in a curve of white sound—
an upturned river, fat with rain
dense with crushed water, a sideways pull
that draws the whole world.

Up close, you can feel a wet gale
sucking you in, tugging at the trees
whose branches dance away

and my children clamber and call.
I don't worry, they're big now, this is their
place, behind the waterfall
while motherly I stand here
on solid rock, to be someone to wave at
to witness their daring.
Their voices are lost in the clamour
of fractured water, of foam
fragments that change form slowly
as they fall, stretching like gum
in emptiness before smashing, reforming

running away. Through a mask of spray
I see them waving:
grey boy and lilac girl
fading and blurred, aslant
behind the torrent, unfocussed
billion tiny lenses dropping through time
and space, holding this moving shape
together, this strange attractor
through which we grin and gesture.

When my son suddenly hugged me yesterday
he had to stoop—a year ago
I stooped to hug him—and he felt light and cool
as rain on my cheek; then out
of my arms and up to his full height
still growing. And my daughter
though she runs like a child, under her lilac sweater
the shadow of breasts in this light.

The waterfall roars between them and me.
Fluid, unbreakable, a closed gate
of running glass through which
they waver and stand

beyond reach yet visible, mouthing
excitedly, deafened by the sound
of waterforms changing, exploding
escaping, unstoppable, sweeping us all
before it, downstream. And when, surprisingly
they return, shaking the thunder from their brains,
soaked through and laughing, it's like meeting
again, after a journey, after a dream.

Hilary Llewellyn-Williams

Beside the Wye
For Stephen Hanvey, 26 July 1989

Before we pitched, we went to the farmer's wife,
Who showed us the communal tap, and told us
That last Friday looking down from their patio
Over that bend where the lean young sallows
Meet the shallows on the smiling pebbly edge
Of a slow, grey and treacherous middle age,

Two youths appeared: the one to teach
The other to swim, to encourage him down
Deep into the Wye to where a sudden depth
Stirs then strikes and it's simpler to drown
Than wave, where the frogman who pulled up
The news said twenty-five feet. We filled up,

Then camped between two maturing ash-trees,
Swam naked out of sight of the farmer's wife,
Returning to our own fields, psychology, poetry,
The last load from Hay. I admire how you can dive
Into dreams, catch what softness nibbles the flesh.
Wonder, were those archetypes we both heard splash

As we trod the littoral? Think, I should look at
Modern Man in Search of a Soul, and try . . .
But now you talk of a camp-fire, ignoring this tinder
Among the loosestrife, bleached driftwood, dry
And light as balsa; and bring, like sacred ewes,
One on each shoulder, ash-logs that we instead use

As seats up here in this sedge confessional
Where the spark takes without any match, without
Need for old jokes about age, as if the years when
You aimed at a penny and missed, when I shot
And won a trophy, had never come between us.
The ash-trees are Masai listening for hyenas:

We talk through them, through tonight's Prom
Which comes from a palmy distant shell full of glees—
Bravo! Heave-ho! Ping-pong! Talk of Hong Kong
Where you have lived . . . Of the boat people, refugees
Whom I knew . . . A hot-air balloon, almost the shape
Of misery, hangs; till a Phantom gives it a wipe.

We are out of sight of the river, of its ghosts,
Yet know we are caught within the coils of a World
Serpent meander, and as you send me now to Jung's
'Wotan', the storm that by dusk will have hurled
Day down from the nineties is crossing Offa's Dyke,
Bleating upon the Black Mountain, soon like

A crow to descend in low corkscrews. Two herons
Appear from the sallies to inform us the river
Is rising. The radio croaks John Major. The wind
Swings from the ash-top on a rope ladder whoever
Has the courage must climb. We drain red wine, our
Reunion bottle, before the peace turns to minor.

John Greening

Birmingham River

Where's Birmingham river? Sunk.
Which river was it? Two. More or less.

History: we're on our tribal ground. When they
moved in from the Trent, the first English

entered the holdings and the bodies of the people
who called the waters that kept them alive

Tame, *the Dark River*; these English spread their works
southward then westward, then all ways

for thirty-odd miles, up to the damp tips of the thirty-odd
weak headwaters of the Tame. By all of the Tame

they settled, and sat, named themselves after it:
Tomsaetan. And back down at Tamworth, where the river

almost began to amount to something,
the Mercian kings kept their state. Dark

because there's hardly a still expanse of it
wide enough to catch the sky, the Dark River

mothered the Black Country and all but
vanished underneath it, seeping out from the low hills

by Dudley, by Upper Gornal, by Sedgley, by
Wolverhampton, by Bloxwich, dropping morosely

without a shelf or a race or a dip,
no more than a few feet every mile, fattened

a little from mean streams that join at
Tipton, Bilston, Willenhall, Darlaston,

Oldbury, Wednesbury. From Bescot
she oozes a border round Handsworth

where I was born, snakes through the flat
meadows that turned into Perry Barr,

passes through Witton, heading for the city
but never getting there. A couple of miles out

she catches the timeless, suspended
scent of Nechells and Saltley—coal gas,

sewage, smoke—turns and makes off
for Tamworth, caught on the right shoulder

by the wash that's run under Birmingham,
a slow, petty river with no memory of an ancient

name; a river called *Rea*, meaning *river*,
and misspelt at that. Before they merge

they're both steered straight, in channels
that force them clear of the gasworks. And the Tame

gets marched out of town in the policed calm
that hangs under the long legs of the M6.

These living rivers
turgidly watered the fields, gave

drink; drove low-powered mills, shoved
the Soho Works into motion, collected waste

and foul waters. Gave way to steam,
collected sewage, factory poisons. Gave way

to clean Welsh water, kept on collecting
typhoid. Sank out of sight

under streets, highways, the back walls of workshops;
collected metals, chemicals, aquicides. Ceased

to draw lines that weren't cancelled or unwanted; became
drains, with no part in anybody's plan.

Roy Fisher

Boundaries

Trees have come up as far as they can
And stand about uncertainly.
Beyond the thistles of the last field
A stream rises, and a lane links
The few farms.

Maps show the contours of the clays
And fields the justice done to heirs.
Down in the village the stream is boastful
Though it does nothing much up here.
You can walk across it.

Boundaries are what link us, surely,
When neighbours turn together from barren
Pasture, when new walls remember
The passing of patriarchs, the drying
Of shared waters.

As trees send saplings to the valley
And all the lanes wind down again,
As the sun rises and sets, creating
New shadows from the same stone,
We are all one.

Within the exact boundaries of
Our skins, of which one inch beyond
Is Nomad's Lodge, the shivering crevice,
We create friend, daughter, lover.
The map converges.

John Fuller

Brian Boru's Well

This well is holy but looks foul.
I clean it seven times a year,
Shovelling quicklime in the shade.
It fills mysteriously dark red.
Once I found a drowned wheatear
And once an old ram's skull.

How does it rise on top of a hill
And why is it never clear?
By miracle, tradition said:
Instead of springing, the rock shed
A slow continual tainted tear
Since Brian Boru's fall.

It was named by St. Gormgall,
Hermit, lion, poet, seer
And king's confessor. When it bled
He knew his penitent was dead.
He saw millennial daybreak tear
Unwinding from its spool.

Even in drought it will not fail
But bless or curse. Don't interfere!
A bigot sledged the crystal bed:
Next day he shot his son in the head
Wild fowling. I cut outlets there
To keep it drinkable.

High Island pivots on this pool.
If a fly walks on the water
All's well with your friend abroad.
It quenched St. Brendan's thirst on board
When he touched here to pray before
Setting out for Hy Brasil.

Around the random horseshoe wall
I helped a mason to repair,
Pennies, fish-hooks, pins corrode.
A thousand years this carved stone stood
Beside the well, giving it power
To comfort or to heal.

Richard Murphy

Bridge

They watch the river passing through
however slow its oil and scum
because they know there is some place
it must go to,
it has come from.

And any river even this
out of the ever it journeys in
brings to their faces one by one
a time of their own
to reflect upon.

G. F. Dutton

The Brook

Murmuring of the brook in late
summer darkness, after moonset,
as I lay sleepless on the porch cot.
A music extraordinarily variable.
Each passage of water against its stone
sounding a different pitch and rhythm.
It was an uncivilized music in the
foothills of the mountains, continuing
long beyond the endurance of a human
singer, almost beyond the endurance
of a human listener, syllables
of unknown meaning, notes on an
unknown scale. A few fat yellow
stars above the northern horizon.
Without art, the song was perfectly
artistic. The unmeaning music
and the unknowing listener were one
in the loneliness of those distant
late summer nights in Vermont.
Truly the music meant nothing,
no intimation, which was why
I liked it so much, my brook
murmuring all night in the darkness,
and I meant nothing, and I liked that too.

Hayden Carruth

The Brook

Seated once by a brook, watching a child
Chiefly that paddled, I was thus beguiled.
Mellow the blackbird sang and sharp the thrush
Not far off in the oak and hazel brush,
Unseen. There was a scent like honeycomb
From mugwort dull. And down upon the dome

Of the stone the cart-horse kicks against so oft
A butterfly alighted. From aloft
He took the heat of the sun, and from below.
On the hot stone he perched contented so,
As if never a cart would pass again
That way; as if I were the last of men
And he the first of insects to have earth
And sun together and to know their worth.
I was divided between him and the gleam,
The motion, and the voices, of the stream,
The waters running frizzled over gravel,
That never vanish and for ever travel.
A grey flycatcher silent on a fence
And I sat as if we had been there since
The horseman and the horse lying beneath
The fir-tree-covered barrow on the heath,
The horseman and the horse with silver shoes,
Galloped the downs last. All that I could lose
I lost. And then the child's voice raised the dead.
'No one's been here before' was what she said
And what I felt, yet never should have found
A word for, while I gathered sight and sound.

Edward Thomas

A Brook in the City

The farmhouse lingers, though averse to square
With the new city street it has to wear
A number in. But what about the brook
That held the house as in an elbow-crook?
I ask as one who knew the brook, its strength
And impulse, having dipped a finger length
And made it leap my knuckle, having tossed
A flower to try its currents where they crossed.
The meadow grass could be cemented down
From growing under pavements of a town;

The apple trees be sent to hearth-stone flame.
Is water wood to serve a brook the same?
How else dispose of an immortal force
No longer needed? Staunch it at its source
With cinder loads dumped down? The brook was thrown
Deep in a sewer dungeon under stone
In fetid darkness still to live and run—
And all for nothing it had ever done
Except forget to go in fear perhaps.
No one would know except for ancient maps
That such a brook ran water. But I wonder
If from it being kept forever under
The thoughts may not have risen that so keep
This new-built city from both work and sleep.

Robert Frost

The Charles River (1)

The sycamores throw shadows on the Charles,
as the fagged insect splinters, drops and joins
the infinite that scatters loosening leaves,
the long-haired escort and his short-skirted girl.
The black stream curves as if it led a lover—
my blood is pounding; in workaday times,
I take cold comfort from its heart elation,
its endless handstand round the single I,
the pumping and thumping of my overfevered wish . . .
For a week my heart has pointed elsewhere:
it brings us here tonight, and ties our hands—
if we leaned forward, and should dip a finger
into this river's momentary black flow,
infinite small stars would break like fish.

Robert Lowell

'Clunton and Clunbury'

Clunton and Clunbury,
  Clungunford and Clun,
Are the quietest places
  Under the sun.

In valleys of springs of rivers,
  By Ony and Teme and Clun,
The country for easy livers,
  The quietest under the sun,

We still had sorrows to lighten,
  One could not be always glad,
And lads knew trouble at Knighton
  When I was a Knighton lad.

By bridges that Thames runs under
  In London, the town built ill,
'Tis sure small matter for wonder
  If sorrow is with one still.

And if as a lad grows older
  The troubles he bears are more,
He carries his griefs on a shoulder
  That handselled them long before.

Where shall one halt to deliver
  This luggage I'd lief set down?
Not Thames, not Teme is the river,
  Nor London nor Knighton the town:

'Tis a long way further than Knighton,
  A quieter place than Clun,
Where doomsday may thunder and lighten
  And little 'twill matter to one.

                    A. E. Housman

Composed upon Westminster Bridge, September 3, 1802

Earth has not anything to show more fair:
Dull would he be of soul who could pass by
A sight so touching in its majesty:
This City now doth, like a garment, wear
The beauty of the morning; silent, bare,
Ships, towers, domes, theatres, and temples lie
Open unto the fields, and to the sky;
All bright and glittering in the smokeless air.
Never did sun more beautifully steep
In his first splendour, valley, rock, or hill;
Ne'er saw I, never felt, a calm so deep!
The river glideth at his own sweet will:
Dear God! the very houses seem asleep;
And all that mighty heart is lying still!

William Wordsworth

Concord River

The turtles on the ledges of July
Heard our approach and splashed. Now in the mud
Lie like the memory of fecund summer
Their buried eggs. The river, colder now,
Has other, autumn tales to carry on
Between the banks where lovers used to lie.

Lovers, or boys escaped from yard and farm
To drown in sensual purities of sun—
No matter which; for single fisherman
Casting into the shade, or those absorbed
In human ardor, summer was the same,
Impervious to weariness or alarm.

The fisherman, by craft and love removed
From meanness, has an almanac at home
Saying the season will be brief this year
And ice strike early; yet upon its shelf
The book is no despoiler of this day
In which he moves and ponders, most himself.

That boy, watching for turtles by the shore,
Steeped in his satisfactory loneliness,
If asked could tell us that the sun would set,
Or autumn drive him back to games and school—
Tell us at second-hand, believing then
Only midsummer and the noonstruck pool.

And we, who floated through the sunlit green,
Indolent, voluntary as the dance
Of dragon-flies above the skimming leaves—
For us the landscape and the hour became
A single element, where our drifting silence
Fell twofold, like our shadows on the water.

This is the Concord River, where the ice
Will hold till April: this is the willowed stream
Much threaded by the native cogitators
Who wrote their journals calmly by its shore,
Observing weather and the swing of seasons
Along with personal cosmologies.

Henry Thoreau most nearly learned to live
Within a world his soul could recognize—
Unshaken by accounts of any country
He could not touch with both his hands. He saw
The river moving past the provincial town
And knew each curve of shoreline for his own.

He travelled much, he said—his wayward speech
Sounding always a little insolent,
Yet surer than the rest; they, like ourselves,

Ran off to dabble in a world beyond
While he exalted the geography
He lived each day: a river and a pond.

For him there was no turning of the ear
To rumored urgencies that sought to rouse
The fisher from his pool, the serious child
From his unconscious wandering: the sound
Of desperate enterprises rang to him
Fictive as ghosts upon old Indian ground.

Lover and child and fisherman, alike
Have in their time been native to this shore
As he would have it peopled: all entranced
By such concerns in their perfected hour
That in their lives the river and the tree
Are absolutes, no longer scenery.

Adrienne Rich

Culvert

Stone stepping over,
cushioning arch
of cut and canted
stones, road's instep
riding the dip

of older workings
with the grain of the rock,
weatherings underground,
where water tells
another story

at cross-purposes
to this: bright threads
under memory, that pool
in memory's loss. Here
is a Roman thread,

a forethought of stone.

Roger Garfitt

A Day on the River

It moved so slowly, friendly as a dog
Whose teeth would never bite;
It licked the hand with cool and gentle tongue
And seemed to share its parasites' delight
Who moved upon its back or moored among
The hairy shallows overhung
With natural parasols of leaves
And bubbling birdsong.
Ukuleles twanged and ladies sang
In punts and houseboats vivid as our own
Bold paintings of the Ark;
This was summer's self to any child:
The plop and suck of water and the old
Sweet rankness in the air beguiled
With deft archaic spells the dim
Deliberations of the land,
Dear river, comforting
More than the trailing hand.

The afternoon of sandwiches and flasks
Drifted away.
The breeze across the shivering water grew
Perceptibly in strength. The sun began to bleed.

'Time to go home,' the punctured uncles said,
And back on land

We trembled at the river's faint, low growl
And as birds probed the mutilated sky
We knew that, with the night,
The river's teeth grew sharp
And they could bite.

Vernon Scannell

Dean-bourn, *a rude River in* Devon, *by which sometimes he lived*

Dean-bourn, farewell; I never look to see
Deane, or thy watry incivility.
Thy rockie bottome, that doth teare thy streams
And makes them frantick, ev'n to all extreames;
To my content, I never sho'd behold,
Were thy streames silver, or thy rocks all gold.
Rockie thou art; and rockie we discover
Thy men; and rockie are thy wayes all over.
O men, O manners; Now, and ever knowne
To be *A Rockie Generation!*
A people currish; churlish as the seas;
And rude (almost) as rudest Salvages.
With whom I did, and may re-sojourne when
Rockes turn to Rivers, Rivers turn to Men.

Robert Herrick

Definition of a Waterfall

Not stitched to air or water but to both
A veil hangs broken in concealing truth

And flies in vague exactitude, a dove
Born diving between rivers out of love

In drums' crescendo beat its waters grow
Conceding thunder's pianissimo

Transfixing ancient time and legend where
A future ghost streams in the present air:

From ledge to pool breakneck across rocks
Wild calm, calm chaos skein their paradox

So that excited poise is fiercely dressed
In a long instant's constant flow of rest,

So that this bridegroom and his bride in white
Parting together headlong reunite

Among her trailing braids. The inconstancy
Is reconciled to fall, falls and falls free

John Ormond

Derwent River

                Was it for this
That one, the fairest of all rivers, loved
To blend his murmurs with my nurse's song,
And, from his alder shades and rocky falls,
And from his fords and shallows, sent a voice
That flowed along my dreams? For this, didst thou,
O Derwent! winding among grassy holms
Where I was looking on, a babe in arms,
Make ceaseless music that composed my thoughts
To more than infant softness, giving me
Amid the fretful dwellings of mankind
A foretaste, a dim earnest, of the calm
That Nature breathes among the hills and groves.

William Wordsworth

Dipper

No webbed feet,
but a water bird for all that.

And a gentlemanly one—
he walks on the bottom
of his helter-skelter stream
wearing a white shirt front
and a brown cummerbund.

He hates dry land.
Flying up a twisty stream
he follows the twists
all the way.

When he perches on a stone
it's a wet one.
He stands there, bobbing and bobbing
as though the water's applauding him.

He likes his nest
to be behind a rippling tapestry—
a tapestry? Well,
a waterfall.

Naturally.

Norman MacCaig

Dockland

Cranes standing still, no work for them
No movement, a monument to times past.
Silhouette outlined against a London sky.

Their reflection, mirrored in the waters of a silent dock.
Casting their shadows across the decks of pleasure yachts.

Like a cancer spreading, with unchecked speed,
Wharves, warehouses closed overnight

Transformed, renovated
Not for people who have no place to live,
But for those who with obscene ease,
Sail their yachts whenever they please,
Leaving them moored outside their second homes.
It's all a part of our social disease.

Docks closed,
Once where dock workers played their part,
Shifting cargo, keeping London alive.
Now silence reigns, it is supreme,
Thrusting aside this industrial scene.

Gone now, this way of life,
Testimony to the power of those few,
Whose decisions carry far and wide,
Eroding, encroaching, changing the
Character of our riverside.

Bernie Steer

Downstream Effects: River Stour

*Written in response to the first performance
of 'Downstream—That's Another Story' by
Karen Wimhurst: music and spoken voices
for 'Confluence', Midsummer's Eve 1999,
Buckhorn Weston.*

Water and voices mingled,
Instruments flowing
The odd and quirky effects
Of stories and reminiscence,
Reflected in the music,
Stopping and starting

And winding on downstream
Images swirling,
Disappearing for a moment,
Re-appearing under bridges
That span several lives
The spring, clear and vivid
The stream alive and fed by ditches,
The river, tapping the resource within,
A shared journey in the dappled light
The orchestra of ripples
Hovering in the air,
Each vision, a powerful reminder
Twisting and turning,
Meandering through the meadows of experience
A rite of passage, scored and distilled,
Composed and sketched,
Milled on the river bank,
The weir of music
Overflowing with ideas
Shades and shadows,
The sudden streak
The darting flash of green and blue
Incandescent, in the silver haze
Fishing for minnows, the flute of youth,
Each pike a bassoon
The clarinets, a brace of tench,
Emerging from the shadows
The chubby French horns, bubbling up,
The piccolo, a stickleback
The oboe and cor anglais, dace and bream
Sharp interjections
Silence bent and barbed
The audience hooked
Each cleft resonating within,
A powerful force.

The river done it—the river done it.

James Crowden

The Dowser

With my forked branch of Lebanese cedar
I quarter the dunes like downs and guide
an invisible plough far over the sand.
But how to quarter such shifting acres
when the wind melts their shapes, and shadows
mass where all was bright before,
and landmarks walk like wraiths at noon?
All I know is that underneath,
how many miles no one can say,
an unbroken water-table waits
like a lake; it has seen no bird or sail
in its long darkness, and no man;
not even pharaohs dug so far
for all their thirst, or thirst of glory,
or thrust-power of ten thousand slaves.
I tell you I can smell it though,
that water. I am old and black
and I know the manners of the sun
which makes me bend, not break. I lose
my ghostly footprints without complaint.
I put every mirage in its place.
I watch the lizard make its lace.
Like one not quite blind I go
feeling for the sunken face.
So hot the days, the nights so cold,
I gather my white rags and sigh
but sighing step so steadily
that any vibrance in so deep
a lake would never fail to rise
towards the snowy cedar's bait.
Great desert, let your sweetness wake.

Edwin Morgan

Drouth End

The stream shrank, curdled in its bed;
cows, maddened, scoured salt flanks.

At last, huge thunder-rain struck
scents from the parched fields.

The river swelled, broached banks,
thick tree-boles breasted it,

all night it scaled the bridge piers,
by first light wet the arch.

Fish nestled in hoof-print,
cattle broke bounds through hedge,

for days trod more than they could cud,
hobbled on rot. Milk waned.

Paul Hyland

An Eel

I

The strange part is his head. Her head. The strangely ripened
Domes over the brain, swollen nacelles
For some large containment. Lobed glands
Of some large awareness. Eerie the eel's head.
This full, plum-sleeked fruit of evolution.
Beneath it, her snout's a squashed slipper-face,
The mouth grin-long and perfunctory,
Undershot predatory. And the iris, dirty gold
Distilled only enough to be different
From the olive lode of her body,
The grained and woven blacks. And ringed larger
With a vaguer vision, an earlier eye

55

Behind her eye, paler, blinder,
Inward. Her buffalo hump
Begins the amazement of her progress.
Her mid-shoulder pectoral fin—concession
To fish-life—secretes itself
Flush with her concealing suit: under it
The skin's a pale exposure of deepest eel
As her belly is, a dulled pearl.
Strangest, the thumb-print skin, the rubberized weave
Of her insulation. Her whole body
Damascened with identity. This is she
Suspends the Sargasso
In her inmost hope. Her life is a cell
Sealed from event, her patience
Global and furthered with love
By the bending stars as if she
Were earth's sole initiate. Alone
In her millions, the moon's pilgrim,
The nun of water.

II

Where does the river come from?
And the eel, the night-mind of water—
The river within the river and opposite—
The night-nerve of water?

Not from the earth's remembering mire
Not from the air's whim
Not from the brimming sun. Where from?

From the bottom of the nothing pool
Sargasso of God
Out of the empty spiral of stars

A glimmering person

Ted Hughes

Eels at Night

Finely poised above the crawling Ffornwg
I watch the strange night turbulence of eels,
For eels like sperm thick spawn the river vat,
Inscribing circles on tar-black water,
Their strings of flesh a skein that instinct ties.

The terror of eels is their writhing fleece,—
The corpse that Ffornwg shreds with slow razors.
Into my own shadow I can plunge my hand
And feel the slippery texture of congealing eels
Like a wound opened in myself, our common skin.

Get an eel in the fist they say, and that's money,
But the cold coin that I grasp now surely buys
More than is guessable, but something like knowledge
Of a life joined with mine, gnashing in blood's long pod,
And a joint affirmation of the hollow flesh.

Robert Minhinnick

Embankment at Night, Before the War

Outcasts

. . . At Charing Cross, here, beneath the bridge
Sleep in a row the outcasts,
Packed in a line with their heads against the wall.
Their feet in a broken ridge
Stretched out on the way, and a lout casts
A look as he stands on the edge of this naked stall.

Beasts that sleep will cover
Their face in their flank; so these
Have huddled rags or limbs on the naked sleep.

Save, as the tram-cars hover
Past with the noise of a breeze
And gleam as of sunshine crossing the low black heap,

Two naked faces are seen
Bare and asleep,
Two pale clots swept by the light of the cars.

Foam-clots showing between
The long, low tidal-heap,
The mud-weed opening two pale, shadowless stars.

Over the pallor of only two faces
Passes the gallivant beam of the trams;
Shows in only two sad places
The white bare bone of our shams.

A little, bearded man, peaked in sleeping,
With a face like a chickweed flower.
And a heavy woman, sleeping still keeping
Callous and dour.

Over the pallor of only two places
Tossed on the low, black, ruffled heap
Passes the light of the tram as it races
Out of the deep . . .

On the outer pavement, slowly,
Theatre people pass,
Holding aloft their umbrellas that flash and are bright
Like flowers of infernal moly
Over nocturnal grass
Wetly bobbing and drifting away on our sight.

And still by the rotten row of shattered feet,
Outcasts keep guard.
Forgotten,
Forgetting, till fate shall delete
One from the ward.

The factories on the Surrey side
Are beautifully laid in black on a gold-grey sky.
The river's invisible tide
Threads and thrills like ore that is wealth to the eye.

And great gold midges
Cross the chasm
At the bridges
Above intertwined plasm.

D. H. Lawrence

The Estuary

A light elegant wall waves down
The riverside, for tidiness
Or decoration—this water
Needs little keeping in—but turns
The corner to face the ocean
And thickens to a bastion.

No one can really taste or smell
Where the salt starts but at one point
The first building looks out to sea
And the two sides of the river
Are forced apart by cold light
And wind and different grasses.

I see this now, but at one time
I had to believe that the two
Sides were almost identical.
I was a child who dared not seem
Gloomy. Traversing grey water
From the east side where I was born

And had spent a normal cross life,
To live gratefully with strangers
On the west side, I grinned and clowned.
I did not go back for ages
And became known for cheerfulness
In a house where all was not well.

Grief was a poltergeist that would
Not materialize but broke
Everything. Neither believed in
Nor dreaded, it took one decade
To appear, one to be recognized,
Then cleared the air wonderfully

So that nowadays I am able
To see the estuary as two
Distinct pieces of countryside,
Not a great deal to choose between
Them perhaps but at least different,
Rising normally from two roots.

On one bank, stiff fields of corn grow
To the hilltop, are draped over
It surrealistically.
On the other, little white boats
Sag sideways twice every day
As the sea pulls away their prop.

Patricia Beer

'The factories, bathing in the Moscow river'

The factories, bathing in the Moscow river,
spin cotton; and the broad green gardens stretch alongside it.
The chattering light of the river crests
speaks of culture, rest and water.

The tubercular, foppish, bureaucratic river,
the Lenin hills, above the Neskuchny Gardens which are the
    boring consistency of halva,
are the stamps and postcards, which like ships
carry us now and into the future.

The Oka river has raised an eyebrow,
that's why there's a breeze on the Moscow river.
Her little sister Klyazma's eyelashes flutter,
that's why the ducks swim on the Yauza.

The Moscow river smells like post-office glue,
the bell-mouthed loudspeakers blare out Schubert.
The water is a spray of pinpoints, and the air
is more tender than the frog-skin of air balloons.

Osip Mandelstam
(translated by Richard & Elizabeth McKane)

First Day of September

(Token of love and honour for Patrick Bromby Mace, poet.
Died August 27, 1970)

Walking by this shallow brook,
Desolate for the dead,
By the senses' dispassionate customs
I am befriended.

This appearance of peat-brown water
Slithering under trees
Engages my fancy to account
For light's unaccountable ways.

Those sparklings might be a handful of trinkets
Tossed in some conjuror's game.
These fish-like glittering and flashes
Make havoc of the smooth theme.

Now I see that the overhung water
Is all flicked by strokes
Of rippling silver. But how motionless
The topaz light that glows

Gently, in pieces fallen
Like manna on water and on grass!—
And wafers of the same elucidation
Grace this leafy path.

Leaves. Tawny as Eggars,
As Brimstones yellow.
Autumn? Summer's in the voices
Of the water, whose fellow,

That summer dove, repeats,
Liquid, cool,
Two-and-a-half pleas endlessly;
A servant of ritual.

Yes, nearly un-noticeable
The voices—so slight
A tinkling, a trifling, a plash;
Absorbed and private

As children's talk in bed.
Yet an eavesdropper may feel
The ancient longing for death
As the world and his heart fall still.

Stilled, I look ahead, where the water,
Flattened, loosely spread,
Shines milk-blue and innocent,
By clumps of cress islanded.

I cross. Walk on. This bank
Rises high above the water.
The field on my left's as steep
As a roof. I walk in its gutter.

My sight is suddenly caught—
Down there, through the broken hedge—
By richest blue. The water's
Blue as alkanet!

I clamber down to a gate
Giving on to the stream's bed;
The sprawled water is colourless
And voiceless as the dead.

Beyond there's that shelterless field
Blazing with light . . .
But here's the peace for dazzled day,
To soothe it to its night.

Frances Bellerby

The Fisherman
for Tom Rawling

I cast my mind over the Greta river,
watch a fisherman sign the evening
with a cursive flourish.
He is the image of Alice.

A stalker through riverbank dark,
under a sudden showering of dew.
His feet usurp the ancient right of eyes;
they tell the ground like a braille.

His milky ghost glides through bramble,
whole skin the opened sensor
of more than touch. The night
has grown bigger than his books,

his preparation for this sleekbacked
ale-darkness, the mirror shards of water.

When it's finished, he'll gladly talk,
how he treasures his privilege.

How it is not so much
the pale torpedo he lays neatly
on the riverside, dead, so diminished,
but the stealth to steal a glance

beyond the looking-glass, where
the trembling whorl wobbles and breaks.
Bright-eyed, he says it never shows
the stamp of any world he knows.

Martyn Crucefix

Five Rivers

Southward from Whitehaven, where cliffs of coal
Slant like shale to the low black mole,
The railway canters along the curving shore
Over five rivers, which slowly pour
On the steps of the shingle where the grey gulls bask
EHEN and CALDER, IRT and MITE and ESK.

The EHEN twists and flicks its fin
Red as rhubarb beneath the grey skin,
For its veins are stained with the blood of the ore
Of the mines of Egremont and Cleator Moor.
Here drill and navvy break the stone
And hack the living earth to the bone;
Blood spurts like water from the stricken rock.
Seeps into drain and gully and trickles to the beck.
Green herringbones of watercresses ride
On the tilt and tug of the red tide;
Bladderwrack, thrift and salty turf
Crust over cobbles at the edge of the pink surf.

The introspective CALDER hums to the pebbles
A memory of plainsong and choirboys' trebles,
Of collect and introit, creed and antiphon,
Of cistercians in the abbey of blood-red stone,
Where now tarpaulin and sheet lead shield
Groined roof and cloister and stoup from the wild
Weather of time, and the wall ferns spread
Where once the praying lamp hung before the holy bread.

The IRT comes from Wastdale, the land of the screes,
Of bracken up to your waist and ham-and-egg teas,
Of men who remember Will Ritson, the biggest liar
That ever lived, who sit by the fire
And laugh their inherited laughs at the talk
Of hounds with wings of eagles sniffing the lake.

The MITE, the tyke, lollops along
Like a blue-haired collie with a dribbling tongue,
The children's plaything as they ride the toy train
That runs beneath the rocks in a hawthorn lane,
Where dog-daisy, dogrose and stiff dog-grass
Bark at the wheels as the whistling truckloads pass.

But the ESK comes from the narrowest dale
Where statesmen meet at the Woolpack for a glass of ale
And a crack about herdwicks or a cure for the tick
And how some fool has broken his neck on the rock.
The ESK knows the stonechat and the parsley fern
And breaks like a bottle at every turn,
And bursts on the boulders and froths like beer,
Runs solid as glass and green and clear,
Till it mixes with MITE and IRT in the marsh,
Where roman cement and arches teach
Of the galleys that came to Ravenglass
Bearing the invaders with helmets of brass.
Where the plover creaks and the curlew whines,
The rivers ferret among the dunes,
Till the channels burst through a gap in the sand
Like a three-pronged pitchfork jabbed in the flank of the land.

Brown clouds are blown against the bright fells
Like celtic psalms from drowned western isles.
The slow rain falls like memory
And floods the becks and flows to the sea,
And there on the coast of Cumberland mingle
The fresh and the salt, the cinders and the shingle.

Norman Nicholson

Flat Rock

Streams divided (around a boulder-cluster or
barge) heal right back together:

gravity's bed takes it all one way, the same
water the substance of distance, subsequent

occasions: water shaken white over
rapids-stones downstream bursts white again

into falls-holes, a permanent eventuum
that takes a name—falls, of course, but

Blank Falls if people stare there, and
this water wrinkles later on through a

sluice so fast people stop to think
about it: Streaking Sluice names that place:

later still this stream spreads out flat over
a shallows-wide ledge-bed, a swim you can
get all the way into almost without getting wet.

A. R. Ammons

Flood

We live in the promise of miraculous lakes:
Dagenham, Greenwich, Wapping, the Isle of Dogs.

'When the siren sounds, those in the blue environs
Should proceed immediately to non-risk zones.'

Spring tides, high winds: for days we can hear
Of nothing else, our eyes bright with disaster,

Our dreams a chronicle of *mountaing anarchie,*
The river-folke frantick, shippës trappt in trees.

And the dove we sent out, when it came back,
Had the brown glaze of estuaries on its beak.

In our dreams no sandbags hold back the flood:
We would bring the whole world down if we could.

Blake Morrison

Floods

Bright as meringues, the swans sweep
sideways down the passionate water.

The boathouse punts are magnetized,
and the rain scores a bull's-eye every time.

There is a bank of froth against the bridge.
It has thrown in the sponge . . .

The flood shines like Occam's razor.
Every quibble returns to the torrent,

and even the slow digressions at our feet
are part of an overall argument.

They cover all the points of grass.
What single-minded brilliance,

what logic!
Not one of us can look away.

                              Craig Raine

A Flowing River

You are lovely as a river
under tranquil skies—
There are imperfections
but a music overlays them—

telling by how dark a bed
the current moves
to what sea that shines
and ripples in my thought

    William Carlos Williams

The Ford

The ploughman stops his wagon at the fore
And sees the brook a river running o'er;
He tries the depth and progs his whip about;
The timid maiden sees the waters out
And asks the ploughman's aid to ride across;
The boy rides fearless on the foremost horse;
The maiden trembles while she keeps her seat

And screams to see the water at her feet;
Fear brings the deepest blushes on her face,
The wagon-boat swims in the deepest place,
The boy holds fast to see the floating tray
And thinks the horses will be swam away;
But soon they gain the side, a merry throng,
And lose their fears and talk and drive along.

John Clare

Fording the Flooded Goldie River

Clamped to the log by the current
Stream breaking over my pack,
Fighting edging across,
Footholds wash out, felt
My body give way: to be
Swept beneath log and downstream,
Down the rocks, to the gorge.
Looked up from the rush of the torrent—
Sunlight in fir-boughs,
Midges in a sunpatch, a bird breaking up,
Cloud on the ridge,
Sky
Blue
I fought death:
        got across it
            alone.

Gary Snyder

Forest Pools

They dream here,
These pools, deep
In quiet fern.
All day they sleep
Still, clear,
Until stars return
And dusk bedims
The glades.

All day the moorhen skims
The waters, green
With lilied weeds,
And dragonflies, blue-mantled, shake
The clustering blades
Of rushes,
As they dart between
Fringing bushes
And reeds.

All day young trout leap
And ripples break
Among the willow beds
Where meadow-sweet and chervil lean
Blossomed heads.

All day,
Mirrored in light,
These pools dream till night;
Then they wake.

Leonard Clark

'Gentle Brent, I used to know you'

Gentle Brent, I used to know you
   Wandering Wembley-wards at will,
Now what change your waters show you
   In the meadowlands you fill!
Recollect the elm-trees misty
And the footpaths climbing twisty
Under cedar-shaded palings,
   Low laburnum-leaned-on railings,
Out of Northholt on and upward to the heights of Harrow hill.

John Betjeman
from Middlesex

Gray Wagtail

It must be summer—you're wearing
your black gorget
above your sulphury shirt front.

You dip and dip and go on dipping
your tail, then shuttlecock up
(death of a fly)
and parachute down again
on to your watery stone.
It's necklaced with bubbles.

No gossip you. You're too busy
dip-dip-dipping your tail—ah,
you're off
in four looping, airy bounds,
hurdling nothing,
to another watery stone
that wears a Beau Brummel jabot of foam
at its throat.

But you put it to shame, little dude.
You're the eight-inch spectacular
in the summery river's
fashion show.

Norman MacCaig

Green River

Green silk, or a shot silk, blue
Verging to green at the edges,
The river reflects the sky
Alas. I wish that its hue
Were the constant green of its sedges
Or the reeds it is floating by.

It reflects the entrances, dangers,
Exploits, vivid reversals
Of weather over the days.
But it learns to make these changes
By too many long rehearsals
Of overcasts and greys.

So let it take its station
Less mutably. Put it to school
Not to the sky but the land.
This endless transformation,
Because it is beautiful,
Let some of it somehow stand.

But seeing the streak of it quiver
There in the distance, my eye
Is astonished and unbelieving.
It exclaims to itself for ever:
This water is passing by!
It arrives, and it is leaving!

Donald Davie

Guests of Silence

*1. Images made and unmade by
the River Wye above Tintern*

Sheer above the river, cliffs.
Stroke upon stroke the current
cleaves rock.
Water builds as it breaks.
Tall above cliffs, trees.

Wrinkled like the mother
first imagined in stone,
an ancient face that is not
for one moment the same.

Now it looks up
and is eaten away: a gargoyle
made of water, spouting.
Vortex. Whirl of galaxies.
Circle on circle
shatters and shapes.

        Ripple,
dint in armour
of black-bright scales.
Mailed crusaders lie in the long bed
silvery-dark.
History is a shadow roughing
the smooth skin.
Bubbles of air and light.

Glaciers crawl down the valley.
Lava erupts through a crack in the earth
and bears down, down.

The river is full
and still has room for the sky.

Lines and nets of grass
hang tangled from branches.
And the river is itself a tree
growing along the ground,
bark-ridged,
feeding with millions of leaves.

Cold, winter-blue,
Alder-green under floodmarks.
Mud colours, a sheen
of red earth.

Suddenly
a coin of light
minted this moment,
a stroke of shadow.

So the world's likeness
appears on the canvas,
and washes out.

Crumbled and carried down,
the red earth is Adam's clay.
A wallowing mudbank
is the beached ark.

The water-face waits
desolate
for the shadow of the dove.

Such bareness
water is, a truth
too slippery-quick to grasp,
skin-taut and bodiless
spirit, and to the poet
who comes despairing of his mind
a companion
that murmurs of the source

and infant spring,
and flows with him, and is his life.

The river fattens the lowlands
with silt, gurgles
to plainchant, whispers
under aisles raised on green lees
to the god of light.

        Such sad music
the human ear shapes,
hearing in the one flow
sighs of a multitude
falling one by one.

Otter and water-rat dive,
shaped to rhythms that slip
the word-knot,
the quaver.

        So bare,
yet utter.
Channel of word and song.

Water from mountain—
mother of rivers,
fleet daughter,
breaker and builder
of the parent ground.

Sweet-salt self
cleaving and raising,
sheer below cliffs
stroke on stroke
the river is

Jeremy Hooker

Heaven

If I imagine Heaven
It is a place where stones are
But no angels.
Over the stones flows
Continuously
The clearest water.
Light lies on the water
Like a sightless eye
Without flicker or ripple,
The stones so deep
The finger of knowledge cannot touch them.
There is a sky
But no celestial music:
A silence only,
So cloudless and remote
A single bird would bring the world with it.

Michael Cullup

Heraclitus on Rivers

Nobody steps into the same river twice.
The same river is never the same
Because that is the nature of water.
Similarly your changing metabolism
Means that you are no longer you.
The cells die; and the precise
Configuration of the heavenly bodies
When she told you she loved you
Will not come again in this lifetime.

You will tell me that you have executed
A monument more lasting than bronze;
But even bronze is perishable.
Your best poem, you know the one I mean,

The very language in which the poem
Was written, and the idea of language,
All these things will pass away in time.

Derek Mahon

'How shy the attraction'

How shy the attraction
of simple rain to east wind
on the dry east side
of the Neversummer Mountains.
Each afternoon clouds sidle in
just so, but rain is seldom.
Here what they call the water table
is more like a shooting star.
Streams that surface in the spring
are veins of fool's gold.
The water we count on
is run-off from high snows
gone underground.
The rest, the rain,
is a tinker's damn.

James Galvin
from Water Table

Hudson River School
for Dorothy and Bill

We drove to the river to see if the shad were rising
Down vistas the painters once flooded with Claudian gold:
The uncompleted spring was still dividing
Shadow-pied acres between the sun and cloud.

77

As the heat flushed through, you could feel the power of summer
Waiting to overtake the spring only half-begun:
'Where are the fishers?' we asked a woman there,
'You'll see them,' she said, 'once the shad are beginning to run.'

They were not running today here, and the lines
Casting infrequently out from coverts along the shore,
Were merely the first and desultory signs
Of what must turn fever and fervour as more and more

Shad thronged the channels—shad that once filled the fords
In such abundance, you could not ride through
Without treading on them. They have outlasted the herds
Of buffalo, the pigeon flocks that even the painters knew

Only by hearsay, for their retrospective gold
Was painting a loss already. We turned to climb
Out of the valley: Van Winkle's mountains showed
Heaped massively up along the horizon line:

As the hills rose around us we began to see—
Only a few at first, then flare on flare
The blossoms that blew from the shadbush, tree on tree,
Whitening the crests in the currents of the air:

The shadblow that comes when the fish are coming
—Spring brings a yearly proof the legend is true—
Told plainly that plenitude could not be long
In reaching the valley to foison the river anew.

Charles Tomlinson

78

Hundred River

in memory of Adam Johnson, 1965–1993

We came to Hundred River through a slow October,
    when earth is scented with everybody's past;
when late scabbed blackberries harden into devil's scars,
    untasted apples rot to bitter toffee.

Across reed-beds a track of blackened railway-sleepers,
    a plank-bridge lapped by barely-stirring water;
swans gargling silently in their fine indifference;
    above, a sky of urgent discursive geese.

Now the year has turned again and I am alone here,
    where willow-herb's dry white whiskers drift over
the brick-red spikes of sorrel and the gossiping reeds;
    and the river sullen, muddied after rain.

No movement in the woods but stealthy growth of fungus,
    hesitant leaf-drop, distant scuttle of deer:
in one marbled, stained oak-leaf I sense gigantic change,
    and in the drizzle feel the season fracture.

Neil Powell

Hungry Thames

Hungry Thames, I walk over the bridge
half-scared you'll whittle me down

where the brown water is eager
and tipped with foam.

You sigh and suck. You lick at the steps
you would like to come up.

Hungry Thames, we feed you on concrete,
orange-peel, polystyrene cups,

79

we hold our kids by a handful of clothing
to let them look at your dimples,

your smiling waters. We should hold them tighter,
these are whirlpools, this is hunger

lashing its tail in the mud, deep down
where the river gets what it wants.

Helen Dunmore

Huntingdonshire Eclogues

I
Here it begins, with the rains of December
that emboss our new north-facing panes and play tom-tom
on the polythene skin across our porch footings.

Like a breath of the primeval: savagely alone,
confronting the spray from Kinder Downfall, or
New Year's Eve paralytic among the Trafalgar Square

fountains . . . Just negative ions, I suppose, making
the stone lions whimper in the subterranean passageways
of my past. 'Past!', our broken guttering echoes.

The water table must have been steadily rising all today—
a thought as cold as quicksilver threading a glass capillary.
The earth mother has lowered her pendulous warm front,

to lean so close above the bed where her water babies lie
that we may be cut off by our own daughter's bed-time.
Darkness is rolling in and the builders have all gone home.

They built the house across the lane on the site of a pond,
our neighbour tells us, and laughs at the thought that one day
it will inseminate that city couple's barren double brick . . .

Behind them, a single field of darkness stretches hedgelessly
towards the Great Ouse. Our 'common stream', as brown
as a common hare, hides in its form there. It has been known

to close the A45. No traffic down the lane tonight,
except a pig-farmer's tractor trundling autumn slurry
away to spread, great wheels scattering pearls of muck.

John Greening

If Anything Will Level with You Water Will

Streams shed out of mountains in a white rust
(such the abomination of height)
slow then into upland basins or high marsh

and slowing drop loose composed figurations
on big river bottoms
or give the first upward turn from plains:

that's for modern streams: if sediment's
lithified it
may have to be considered ancient, the result of

a pressing, perhaps lengthy, induration:
old streams from which the water's
vanished are interesting, I mean that

kind of tale,
water, like spirit, jostling hard stuff around
to make speech into one of its realest expressions:

water certainly is interesting (as is spirit) and
small rock, a glacial silt, just as much so:
but most pleasurable (magma & migma) is

rock itself in a bound slurp or spill
or overthrust into very recent times:
there waterlike stone, those heated seekings &

goings, cools to exact concentration, I
mean the telling's unmediated:
the present allows the reading of much

old material: but none of it need be read:
it says itself (and
said itself) so to speak perfectly in itself.

A. R. Ammons

In Avon

In Spring we can taste the river
as far as our bed.
We dream of frogs and silt
in the brackish dark,
then wake in the daylight
prepared for a transformation.

Or we sit in the loam-flavoured shadows
under the trees
and watch for hours, for what the river brings:
the flat eyes and glimpses of bronze
in the bottleglass weeds,
the rumours of ourselves that come in waves,
the spun lights and splinters of naming.

The river is a life we do not use:
the dreams we half-remember, then forget,
a shimmer of sequins and tinsel
dissolving, like a vein of starch and yeast
we take for love.

Away from the bank, we sit in the standstill of home,
with nothing to wait for, and nothing to understand;
the river is flowing away and remaining in place,
sifted by summer, darkened by foxes and owls;
in autumn the leaves bleed out through a wavering skin,
seed finds its level, fishbones and fleece decay.

All winter it changes. We find it again and again.

John Burnside

In the Backs

Too many of the dead, some I knew well,
Have smelt this unforgotten river smell,
Liquid and old and dank;
And on the tree-dark, lacquered, slowly passing stream
Have seen the boats come softly as in dream
Past the green bank.
So Camus, reverend sire, came footing slow
Three hundred years ago,
And Milton paced the avenue of trees
In miracle of sun and shade as now,
The fresh-attempted glorious cadences
Behind his youthful brow.

Milton and Chaucer, Herbert, Herrick, Gray,
Rupert, and you forgotten others, say—
Are there slow rivers and bridges where you have gone away?
What has your spirit found? What wider lot?
Some days in spring do you come back at will,
And tread with weightless feet the ancient ground?
O say, if not,
Why is this air so sacred and so still?

Frances Cornford

Inscription
for a Fountain on a Heath

This Sycamore, oft musical with bees,—
Such tents the Patriarchs loved! O long unharmed
May all its aged boughs o'er-canopy
The small round basin, which this jutting stone
Keeps pure from falling leaves! Long may the Spring,
Quietly as a sleeping infant's breath,
Send up cold waters to the traveller
With soft and even pulse! Nor ever cease
Yon tiny cone of sand its soundless dance,
Which at the bottom, like a Fairy's page,
As merry and no taller, dances still,
Nor wrinkles the smooth surface of the Fount.
Here twilight is and coolness: here is moss,
A soft seat, and a deep and ample shade.
Thou may'st toil far and find no second tree.
Drink, Pilgrim, here; Here rest! and if thy heart
Be innocent, here too shalt thou refresh
Thy Spirit, listening to some gentle sound,
Or passing gale or hum of murmuring bees!

Samuel Taylor Coleridge

Kingfisher

Brown as nettle-beer, the stream
Shadow-freckled, specked with sun
Slides between the trees.

Not a ripple breaks in foam;
Only the frilled hedge-parsley falls
White upon the ground.
No insect drills the air; no sound
Rustles among the reeds.
Bird and leaf and thought are still
When shot from the blue a kingfisher
Flashes between the ferns—
Jewelled torpedo sparkling by
Under the bridge and gone;
Yet bright as a bead behind the eye,
The image blazes on.

Phoebe Hesketh

Kingfisher

That kingfisher jewelling upstream
seems to leave a streak of itself behind it
in the bright air. The trees
are all the better for its passing.

It's not a mineral eater, though it looks it:
It doesn't nip nicks out of the edges
of rainbows. —It dives
into the burly water, then, perched
on a Japanese bough, gulps
into its own incandescence

a wisp of minnow, a warrior stickleback.
—Or it vanishes into its burrow, resplendent
Samurai, returning home
to his stinking slum.

Norman MacCaig

The Kingfisher

So when the Shadows laid asleep
From underneath these Banks do creep,
And on the River as it flows
With *Eben Shuts* begin to close;
The modest *Halcyon* comes in sight,
Flying betwixt the Day and Night;
And such an horror calm and dumb,
Admiring Nature does benum.

The viscous Air, wheres'ere She fly,
Follows and sucks her Azure dy;
The gellying Stream compacts below,
If it might fix her shadow so;
The stupid Fishes hang, as plain
As *Flies* in *Chrystal* overt'ane;
And Men the silent *Scene* assist,
Charm'd with the *Saphir-winged Mist*.

Andrew Marvell

The Launch

That Saturday, launch of the yard's last tug
We stood watching from the opposite bank,
Among willowherb, bushes, crunched cinders.
We stood, to get a view, in the tips of our shoes.

Above our heads the railway viaduct
Thundered occasionally as timetabled.
Out of sight, upstream, the meadows flourished,
As fresh each summer, screens of alders
Dipped between the fishermen
Who waited for the silent shoals of roach.
Down here fish would choke, grow thin with rust
Out of the dock's subsistence and iron litter.
Over there some men talked, about to be unemployed
After the ceremony. I could see your mother,
Cautiously dispossessed in an idle corner
Among riveters' stockades like a cabbage white
In her pale coat, never properly alighting there.
I wondered what they would do having no work,
Even your father, and yet they all seemed happy
As at a wedding, tulip coloured hats,
Supertax suits, wide ties of directors.
We watched from the other side. It was a carnival
In honour of that animal trunk of metal,
A giving of something into something else,
A sort of finish that was, it seems now, both ripeness
And goodbye, for the yard, the people, for the ship.
Once its decks were built it would tow out
All the purpose they could never repeat
Yet which had strong bearings and good shape.
Somehow I knew that then, seeing them laugh,
Seeing the ribbon swing its champagne lace
Breaking into the bows, as if that soft
Light enough gesture
Caused us to feel the river's membrane winded.
Our eyes slid with the keel
Which took no time but emptied a ripple up
Higher than the workshops, one side-wave
As it slid in sideways like a knife, halving
The narrow waterway as we cheered.
Under bridges, further towards the town,
The river lay, a sleeve of crooked iron.

Paul Mills

Liffey Water

Green, where Thames is grey
   or mud-murk hued,
this winding scarf of water
   bears its living load

of history in a ghostly barge.
   Under needle-pointed stars
at night, by warehouse blocks
   and Dublin's crackling bars,

the rubbing waters chafe at brick
   to let you know what you must solve:
how every mortal thing there is
   must soon dissolve.

William Oxley

'Like Rain it sounded till it curved'

Like Rain it sounded till it curved
And then I knew 'twas Wind—
It walked as wet as any Wave
But swept as dry as sand—
When it had pushed itself away
To some remotest Plain
A coming as of Hosts was heard
That was indeed the Rain—
It filled the Wells, it pleased the Pools
It warbled in the Road—
It pulled the spigot from the Hills
And let the Floods abroad—

It loosened acres, lifted seas
The sites of Centres stirred
Then like Elijah rode away
Upon a Wheel of Cloud.

Emily Dickinson

Long Nanny Burn
Beadnell Bay

This place changes with every tide;
Buries the wheels and springs of World War II machines,
Twisting them deeper under the tons of sandhills
Like an obscene dream inside.

Down where the river scoops low, wind smooths, time passes,
Mounding the dunes up, carving them through from the floodland.
The sky, swept cold blue, sprawls enormously wide here.
Winged skeletons litter the sand.

But week by year, the river is shifting its wash.
It wrestles the irresistible push. The sea,
Its rage contained, inhales; retreats, revealing
Sharp-edged scrap, mud-sunk. Hard memory.

I've watched this, life-long, longer than all life; fighting
River, struggling, tight as a muscle, months; then suddenly strong,
Forcing its straight path through overnight, slicing the sand clean.
Nothing buried lies safe here for long.

Katrina Porteous

Lothian Burn

Up here, scarcely
birdsong even: only

the labials and gutturals
of this burn as it gurgles

downhill, locality of accent
in vowel and consonant,

each circumlocution
through heather and sandstone

traced by inflection
and sharp interjection

until, in a mossy outcrop,
it comes to a glottal stop.

Stewart Conn

The Mill-Water

Only the sound remains
Of the old mill;
Gone is the wheel;
On the prone roof and walls the nettle reigns.

Water that toils no more
Dangles white locks
And, falling, mocks
The music of the mill-wheel's busy roar.

Pretty to see, by day
Its sound is naught
Compared with thought
And talk and noise of labour and of play.

Night makes the difference.
In calm moonlight,
Gloom infinite,
The sound comes surging in upon the sense:

Solitude, company,—
When it is night,—
Grief or delight
By it must haunted or concluded be.

Often the silentness
Has but this one
Companion;
Wherever one creeps in the other is:

Sometimes a thought is drowned
By it, sometimes
Out of it climbs;
All thoughts begin or end upon this sound,

Only the idle foam
Of water falling
Changelessly calling,
Where once men had a work-place and a home.

Edward Thomas

Mists over the River

The river-mirror mirrors the cold sky
through mists that tangle sunlight,
the sunlight of early morning,
in their veils veiling

the dark outlines of the shores. But
the necessity, you say, cries
aloud for the adjusting—greater than
song, greater perhaps than all song

While the song, self committed, the river
a mirror swathed in sunlight,
the river in its own body cries out
also, silently

from its obscuring veils. You
insist on my unqualified endorsement.
Many years, I see, many years
of reading have not made you wise.

William Carlos Williams

Mother Anthony's

Looking for the well in the wood
the named well in the named wood,
looking for a source, a spell
of water from rock, from soil
from the veins of trees—
and never quite finding it

we visited, we revisited
in all seasons, with the wood blown
and bare, or sappy and plush
full of voices, to discover
a stream without source, whose source
shifted from rock to swamp
to cornfield. What we found

wasn't the named well, but something
unnameable. A tingle beneath skin,
the way all paths led downwards
crouched under boughs. And the stream
stone cold, with a crushed taste.

Once there were hares racing
at dusk up and down the hill
as we approached, oblivious to us.
Once a thunderstorm
that pelted us from the trees
into the parched stubble of the fields.

We visited, we revisited.
We found a bottle buried in a pool,
old bubbled glass. Sometimes we drink
from it, toast Mother Anthony,
looking for what was lost.

Hilary Llewellyn-Williams

The Names of the Sea-Trout

He who would seek her in the clear stream,
Let him go softly, as in a dream,
He who would hold her well,
Let him first whisper the spell
Of her names,

The silver one, the shimmering maiden,
The milkwhite-throated bride,
The treasure-bringer from the sea,
Leaper of weirs, hurdler to the hills,
The returning native, egg-carrier,
The buxom lass, the wary one,
The filly that shies from a moving shadow,
The darter-away, the restless shiner,
Lurker in alder roots,
The fearful maid,

Night dancer, ring maker,
The one that splinters reflections,
The splasher, the jester, the teaser, the mocker,
The false encourager, tweaker of lures,
The girl who is fasting, destroyer of hopes,
Bender of steel, the breaker, the smasher,
The strong wench, the cartwheeler,
The curve of the world,
She who doesn't want to surrender,
The desired, the sweet one.

When you've spent nights and days
Speaking her names, learning her ways,
Take down your tackle from the shelf,
And your skill. She may give herself
For the whispered spell.

Tom Rawling

Net and River

The old bus, nose to the road like a dog,
takes them all the way to the village
with its one shop and shining river.

The net she picks is green, uncertain
on its skinny pole as she dips it
back and forth, between the weeds,
over the stones and catches a fish.

A fish. A flicker and jump in water,
in air: a flash like memory itself.

Watching its ugly gasp for life,
the river fall from its back in tears,
the unkind swat of its head on stone,
she has to drop it back again

and let the waters close, the ripples spread
wide and wider till they can't be seen,
till the lip of deepest water stops its trembling.

Maura Dooley

Not Drinking Water

Home after years, tonight,
cleaning my teeth,
I taste the water of childhood,
still unfluorided,
tangless, not tepid, quite—
once an apple-slicing chill
by which all quenchings could be placed.

Suddenly minute fear,
not noticing the granary tower
by the old mill pond
that used to dominate the sky round here.
—Dwarfed
a little beyond
some concrete block for storing flour.

The water I've tasted:
shower, river, full of lime,
brine of the eyes,
sweat of her brow,
hard and soft and somewhere sour.
This taste I seem to forget.
I have been thirsty all my life.

Peter Dale

'Now the children are old enough . . .'

Now the children are old enough to see what there is to see
we take them to Tower Bridge and explain how the road lifts up,
how traitors arrived at Traitor's Gate, how this was a brewery

and that was a warehouse, how the river starts many miles inland
and changes and grows, changes and grows, until it arrives here,
London, where we live, then winds past Canary Wharf

(which they've done in school) and out to sea.
Afterwards we lean on the railings outside a café. It's autumn.
The water is speckled with leaves, and a complicated tangle of junk

bumps against the embankment wall: a hank of bright grass,
a rotten bullrush stem, a fragment of dark polished wood.
One of the children asks if people drown in the river, and I think

of Ruth, who was on the *Marchioness*. After her death, I met
someone who had survived. He had been in the lavatory when the
                                                              dredger hit,
and fumbled his way out along a flooded corridor, his shoes

and clothes miraculously slipping off him, so that when he at last
burst into the air he felt that he was a baby again
and knew nothing, was unable to help himself, aghast.

I touch my wife's arm and the children gather round us.
We are the picture of a family on an outing. I love it. I love the river
and the perky tour-boats with their banal chat. I love the snub barges.

I love the whole dazzling cross-hatchery of traffic and currents,
shadows and sun, standing still and moving forward.
The tangle of junk bumps the wall below me again and I look down.

There is Ruth swimming back upstream, her red velvet party dress
flickering round her heels as she twists through the locks
and dreams round the slow curves, slithering on for miles

until she has passed the ponderous diver at Folly Bridge
and the reed-forests at Lechlade, accelerating beneath bridges and
                                            willow branches,
slinking easily among the plastic wrecks and weedy trolleys,

speeding and shrinking and silvering until finally she is sliding uphill
over bright green grass and into the small wet mouth of the earth,
where she vanishes.

Andrew Motion
from Fresh Water *(In Memory of Ruth Haddon)*

October

The October water is like glass and scarcely flows.
Beside the red tree the swan spreads a long wing.
Rose hips too are reflected in the stream
Where the bird's sudden movement has made no sound.

Iris Murdoch

An Offering

We live on the dry surface,
Power our grass short
And play over rich topsoil.
Keep a cap on the old wells,

Afraid to imagine what might echo
Under familiar place-names, or what
If we should stop turning
And pull, and lift the concrete.

My offering to the guardians
Of the thousand covered wells
Lost to mucilage, or filled
With hardcore and paved, my gift

To St. Anne, to Black Annis,
To you nymphs and water deities,
To all trout, snakes, toads, flies
That guard them still, is these

Lines that are bent like steel
Wishing pins—catch them!—words
Spin-gleaming through your legendry,
New-coined; and if you have no wish

For this severed head that sings
Its vaporous red trail
Down into your nursery rhymeless
Black, toss it back.

John Greening

On Sturminster Foot-Bridge

Reticulations creep upon the slack stream's face
    When the wind skims irritably past,
The current clucks smartly into each hollow place
That years of flood have scrabbled in the pier's sodden base;
    The floating-lily leaves rot fast.

On a roof stand the swallows ranged in wistful waiting rows,
    Till they arrow off and drop like stones
Among the eyot-withies at whose foot the river flows:
And beneath the roof is she who in the dark world shows
    As a lattice-gleam when midnight moans.

Thomas Hardy

On the River Avon, near Stratford

He is, of course, the genius of the place,
That is, of midland England, whose flatness
Rescues it from unreasonable beauty;
A pleasant, unremarkable country
Watered by its river Avon, whose source is
The middle point of England, near Naseby.

I knew its reaches well: at least from Evesham
As far as Warwick. Then I was a boy
And it was the summer armadas came over
With the full moon, flying to Birmingham
And back again, unladen, before morning.
I saw the cattle drowsing in the fields,
And black elms ponder over scarcely pacing
Water, while white spokes of light, far off,
Walked on the horizon until All Clear.

And there my boat lay, floating on the water,
Well above Bidford; ready to go on.

The time, like all times, furious; my voyage
Frivolous, without aim, peripheral.
But now I feel its meaning, as I did then,
A realization that a golden age
Exists; at all times, though no age is golden;
And that it is enough to see it once:
A derelict park, receding pastoral,
An intense present, ever caught between
All that must be because of what has been.

David Wright

Otter Out and In

Collison of opposites which pulls the river
plucks the otter through an aperture
and lays and breeds the river, high and low,
through Dipper Mill in her absorbing beauty;

and brings us running from the field
and throws and cleaves us into shadows
arm in arm and apart upon the water;
and flexes the otter in and out the water.

The whole river transforms upon an otter.
Now and gone, sometimes we see him
swimming above the fish—half-of-the-air,
half-of-the-darkness—when he dives,

a duck-flip into darkness, creep
close to the edge and closer. There are times
when water's attentiveness
is tight enough to walk on

and we came so strangely
out of the darkness to this world
of watersounds colliding slowly,
out and in and disappear in darkness . . .

Alice Oswald

Penmaen Pool
For the Visitors' Book at the Inn

Who long for rest, who look for pleasure
Away from counter, court, or school
O where live well your lease of leisure
But here at, here at Penmaen Pool?

You'll dare the Alp? you'll dart the skiff?
Each sport has here its tackle and tool:
Come, plant the staff by Cadair cliff;
Come, swing the sculls on Penmaen Pool.

What's yonder? —Grizzled Dyphwys dim:
The triple-hummocked Giant's Stool,
Hoar messmate, hobs and nobs with him
To halve the bowl of Penmaen Pool.

And all the landscape under survey,
At tranquil turns, by nature's rule,
Rides repeated topsyturvy
In frank, in fairy Penmaen Pool.

And Charles's Wain, the wondrous seven,
And sheep-flock clouds like worlds of wool,
For all they shine so, high in heaven,
Shew brighter shaken in Penmaen Pool.

The Mawddach, how she trips! though throttled
If floodtide teeming thrills her full,
And mazy sands all water-wattled
Waylay her at ebb, past Penmaen Pool.

But what's to see in stormy weather,
When grey showers gather and gusts are cool?
Why, raindrop-roundels looped together
That lace the face of Penmaen Pool.

Then even in weariest wintry hour
Of New Year's month or surly Yule
Furred snows, charged tuft above tuft, tower
From darksome darksome Penmaen Pool.

And ever, if bound here hardest home,
You've parlour-pastime left and (who'll
Not honour it?) ale like goldy foam
That frocks an oar in Penmaen Pool.

Then come who pine for peace or pleasure
Away from counter, court, or school,
Spend here your measure of time and treasure
And taste the treats of Penmaen Pool.

Gerard Manley Hopkins

The Poet as Spirit of the River

My first druid of nature,
lone man knowing music of
curlew, whistle of otter,
taught me the river and love
of the fish: lone man in small
southern town, I saw your eyes
mild as mist: took as symbols
your animals: gulls that rise

up screaming in the inland,
crow of cock pheasant, long and
copper to my ears, after
your describing them: your hands
from feather, bone and fire wire
fashioning the flies to fish
just wanting from me the truth
and may God grant you your wish.

In the bright night of two moons,
moon on water, moon on tree,
back from the devious ways
of poetry, hail to me.
In the bright night of two moons
at musical riverbends
we shall pray that there may be
no deserting between friends.

Michael Hartnett

The Porch over the River

In the dusk of the river, the wind
gone, the trees grow still—
the beautiful poise of lightness,
the heavy world pushing toward it.

Beyond, on the face of the water,
lies the reflection of another tree,
inverted, pulsing with the short strokes
of waves the wind has stopped driving.

In a time when men no longer
can imagine the lives of their sons
this is still the world—
the world of my time, the grind

of engines marking the country
like an audible map, the high dark
marked by the flight of men,
lights stranger than stars.

The phoebes cross and re-cross
the openings, alert
for what may still be earned
from the light. The whippoorwills

begin, and the frogs. And the dark
falls, again, as it must.
The look of the world withdraws
into the vein of memory.

The mirrored tree, darkening, stirs
with the water's inward life. What has
made it so?—a quietness in it
no question can be asked in.

Wendell Berry

The Question

I dreamed that, as I wandered by the way,
  Bare Winter suddenly was changed to Spring,
And gentle odours led my steps astray,
  Mixed with a sound of waters murmuring
Along a shelving bank of turf, which lay
  Under a copse, and hardly dared to fling
Its green arms round the bosom of the stream,
But kissed it and then fled, as thou mightest in dream.

There grew pied wind-flowers and violets,
  Daisies, those pearled Arcturi of the earth,
The constellated flower that never sets;
  Faint oxslips; tender bluebells, at whose birth

The sod scarce heaved; and that tall flower that wets—
  Like a child, half in tenderness and mirth—
Its mother's face with Heaven's collected tears,
When the low wind, its playmate's voice, it hears.

And in the warm hedge grew lush eglantine,
  Green cowbind and the moonlight-coloured may,
And cherry-blossoms and white cups, whose wine
  Was the bright dew, yet drained not by the day;
And wild roses, and ivy serpentine,
  With its dark buds and leaves, wandering astray;
And flowers azure, black, and streaked with gold,
Fairer than any wakened eyes behold.

And nearer to the river's trembling edge
  There grew broad flag-flowers, purple pranked with white,
And starry river buds among the sedge,
  And floating water-lilies, broad and bright,
Which lit the oak that overhung the hedge
  With moonlight beams of their own watery light;
And bulrushes, and reeds of such deep green
As soothed the dazzled eye with sober sheen.

Methought that of these visionary flowers
  I made a nosegay, bound in such a way
That the same hues, which in their natural bowers
  Were mingled or opposed, the like array
Kept these imprisoned children of the Hours
  Within my hand,—and then, elate and gay,
I hastened to the spot whence I had come,
That I might there present it! —Oh! to whom?

                                    Percy Bysshe Shelley

Repose of Rivers

The willows carried a slow sound,
A sarabande the wind mowed on the mead.
I could never remember
That seething, steady leveling of the marshes
Till age had brought me to the sea.

Flags, weeds. And remembrance of steep alcoves
Where cypresses shared the noon's
Tyranny; they drew me into hades almost.
And mammoth turtles climbing sulphur dreams
Yielded, while sun-silt rippled them
Asunder . . .

How much I would have bartered! the black gorge
And all the singular nestings in the hills
Where beavers learn stitch and tooth.
The pond I entered once and quickly fled—
I remember now its singing willow rim.

And finally, in that memory all things nurse;
After the city that I finally passed
With scalding unguents spread and smoking darts
The monsoon cut across the delta
At gulf gates . . . There, beyond the dykes

I heard wind flaking sapphire, like this summer,
And willows could not hold more steady sound.

Hart Crane

Rising Damp

A river can sometimes be diverted, but it is a
very hard thing to lose it altogether. (J. G. Head:
paper read to the Auctioneers' Institute, 1907.)

At our feet they lie low,
The little fervent underground
Rivers of London

(Effra, Graveney, Falcon, Quaggy,
Wandle, Walbrook, Tyburn, Fleet)

Whose names are disfigured,
Frayed, effaced.

These are the Magogs that chewed the clay
To the basin that London nestles in.
These are the currents that chiselled the city,
That washed the clothes and turned the mills,
Where children drank and salmon swam
And wells were holy.

They have gone under.
Boxed, like the magician's assistant.
Buried alive in earth.
Forgotten, like the dead.

They return spectrally after heavy rain,
Confounding suburban gardens. They infiltrate
Chronic bronchitis statistics. A silken
Slur haunts dwellings by shrouded
Watercourses, and is taken
For the footing of the dead.

Being of our world, they will return
(Westbourne, caged at Sloane Square,
Will jack from his box),
Will deluge cellars, detonate manholes,
Plant effluent on our faces,
Sink the city

(Effra, Graveney, Falcon, Quaggy,
Wandle, Walbrook, Tyburn, Fleet)

It is the other rivers that lie
Lower, that touch us only in dreams
That never surface. We feel their tug
As a dowser's rod bends to the source below

(Phlegethon, Acheron, Lethe, Styx).

U. A. Fanthorpe

River

'. . . I saw with infinite pleasure the great object of my
mission; the long sought for, majestic Niger, glittering
to the morning sun, as broad as the Thames at Westminster,
and flowing slowly *to the eastward.*' —Mungo Park,
Travels in the Interior Districts of Africa.

The strong image is always the river
was a line for the poem I never wrote
twenty years ago and never have written
of the green Wanganui under its willows
or the ice-blue milky-foaming Clutha
stopping my tremulous teenage heart.

But now when I cross Westminster Bridge
all that comes to mind is the Niger
a river Mungo Park invented for me
as he invented all those African villages
and a certain kind of astonishing silence—
the explorer having done the poet's job
and the poet feeling gratefully redundant.

Fleur Adcock

River

Here the river
closes on twigs, dried weeds
dead wood; has made

a frozen long necrology
of things growing
once, things now
hard as they are.

>Ice/man, old
>illusion yet
>real as cold, you
>petrify reflection:

>I see myself turn
>rigid in your sad
>mirror while I look:

>a flat out-
>line, pale blue
>oval vacancy

circled by your
winter dream, starved
pickerel, pike,
these hungers

and in the centre of my
absent face your summer
dream: green

violence, a latent
hook
locked in the ice.

Margaret Atwood

River

At the turn of the river the language changes,
a different babble, even a different name
for the same river. Water crosses the border,
translates itself, but words stumble, fall back,
and there, nailed to a tree, is proof. A sign

in new language brash on a tree. A bird,
not seen before, singing on a branch. A woman
on the path by the river, repeating a strange sound
to clue the bird's song and ask for its name, after.
She kneels for a red flower, picks it, later
will press it carefully between the pages of a book.

What would it mean to you if you could be
with her there, dangling your own hands in the water
where blue and silver fish dart away over stone,
stoon, stein, like the meanings of things, vanish?
She feels she is somewhere else, intensely, simply because
of words; sings loudly in nonsense, smiling, smiling.

If you were really there what would you write on a postcard,
or on the sand, near where the river runs into the sea?

Carol Ann Duffy

River

in the black gland of the earth
the tiny inkling of a river

put your ear to the river you hear trees
put your ear to the trees you hear the widening
numerical workings of the river

right down a length of whiteness,
under a milky square of light that keeps quite still

the river slows down and goes on

with storm trash clustered on its branches
and paper unfolding underwater
and pairs of ducks swimming over bright grass among flooded
willows

the earth's eye
looking through the earth's bones

carries the moon carries the sun but keeps nothing

Alice Oswald

A River
(For Edward Lowbury)

The line between land and water
Forms itself without thought.
Land ends where on the river
No one can walk,
Though the deep, familiar
Path looks hard as silver,
Though land can be held there
Firm in precise inversion
As an eye holds rock.

Neither side of the river
Is a mountain, and no mind
Hesitates, moving from one
Bank to the other,
To cross the line.
Solid boats grow
In the ploughed slime.
Ducks with their hungry beaks
Break the water.

Where's an end to illusion?
Swans, clusters of pale stems,
Finger the air;
Their tuberous bodies
Flower momentarily.
The river is full of fungi,
Its scabby trunk
Breathes sour putrefaction
Out of the fen.

At night, the land slips softly
Into the river in vague
Columns of light, as the line
Between land and water
Forms in the eye
Of any casual observer
Who crosses the line
Between himself and object
Ceaselessly, without thought.

Anne Stevenson

The River

He is whipping the air into shape;
the flies he has tied
drift dry as a bone.
He has taken an element
in his stride.

He is driving them on,
the waterway horses,
flailing the crop of upcountry spawns.

Beneath is the grain. Splashes
are chaff of whitewater courses.

He has stepped into the same stream
often and recently seen it putrefy.
He has loved a place
he'll feel a need to leave.
They had to milk the good cow dry.

He was making light but not little of
the tarnished hallmark
of the bank, the copper line,
dank overgrowth. He was making
light of midsummer dark

when we were fishing and thinking
with a friend. 'There's a lake,'
wrote a man, 'deep
in the mind of everyone,'
and he was making a mistake.

It's a river.

Peter Fallon

The River

I

Hail sacred spring, whose fruitful stream
  Fattens the flocks, and cloaths the plain,
The melancholy poets theme,
  And solace of the thirsty swain.

II

Thou fly'st, like time, with eager haste;
  Behind thy self thou still dost stay;
Thy stream, like his, is never past,
  And yet is ever on the way.

III

While mankind boasts superior sight,
  With eyes erect the heav'ns to see;
The starry eyes of heav'n delight
  To gaze upon themselves in thee.

IV

A second sun thou dost present,
  And bring new heav'ns before our eyes;
We view a milder firmament,
  And pleas'd, look downward to the skies.

V

Thy streams were once th' impartial test
  Of untaught nature's humble pride,
When by thy glass the nymphs were drest,
  In flow'rs, the honours of thy side.

VI

Of thee they drank, till blushing fruit
  Was ravisht from the tender vine;
And man, like thee, was impollute,
  Till mischief learn'd to mix with wine.

Alexander Pope

The River

And the cobbled water
Of the stream with the trout's indelible
Shadows that winter
Has not erased—I walk it
Again under a clean
Sky with the fish, speckled like thrushes,
Silently singing among the weed's
Branches.
    I bring the heart
Not the mind to the interpretation
Of their music, letting the stream
Comb me, feeling it fresh
In my veins, revisiting the sources
That are as near now
As on the morning I set out from them.

       R. S. Thomas

The River God
of the River Mimram in Hertfordshire

I may be smelly, and I may be old,
Rough in my pebbles, reedy in my pools,
But where my fish float by I bless their swimming
And I like the people to bathe in me, especially women.
But I can drown the fools
Who bathe too close to the weir, contrary to rules.
And they take a long time drowning
As I throw them up now and then in a spirit of clowning.
Hi yih, yippity-yap, merrily I flow,
O I may be an old foul river but I have plenty of go.
Once there was a lady who was too bold
She bathed in me by the tall black cliff where the water runs cold,

So I brought her down here
To be my beautiful dear.
Oh will she stay with me will she stay
This beautiful lady, or will she go away?
She lies in my beautiful deep river bed with many a weed
To hold her, and many a waving reed.
Oh who would guess what a beautiful white face lies there
Waiting for me to smooth and wash away the fear
She looks at me with. Hi yih, do not let her
Go. There is no one on earth who does not forget her
Now. They say I am a foolish old smelly river
But they do not know of my wide original bed
Where the lady waits, with her golden sleepy head.
If she wishes to go I will not forgive her.

Stevie Smith

River History

Even then the river carried cargo,
Saxon corn shipped to storehouses on the Rhine.
Taxes were paid in pepper and cloth by the Easterlings,
the German merchants trading from the Steelyard
demolished in the fire of 1666.
Wharves burned like touchpaper, packed
with resin, sulphur, pitch.
The daily catch between London and Deptford
was salmon, eel, smelt and plaice
but the Port Authority preferred to dine
at the Tavern on the best turtle soup in the City
as they argued the height of the wall to be built
against the Mudlarks, Plunderers and Peterboatmen,
intent on their nightly specialized percentage:
cloves from Zanzibar, mother-of-pearl,
tortoiseshell, South American iodine,
West Indian rum, the heavy iron bottles
of Spanish quicksilver, and, from Ivory House,
the occasional mammoth tusk unfrozen in Siberia.

The Empire expanded, cess-pits were banned,
water grew thick with steamships and sewage
and the docks pushed east out into the marshes,
breaking the horizon with a forest of cranes
that unloaded meat, cloth, tobacco and grain
from countries my school atlas still colours pink.
At the Crutched Friars Deposit Office records were kept
of ships in berth, noted daily
by a row of clerks crouched under gaslight
and seven-foot ceilings. Records were kept
of each member of the Union, the fight to be paid
a tanner an hour and not have to climb each day
on another's back and shout to be chosen.
There was always the army.
The Luftwaffe bombed Surrey Commercial Docks
for fifty-seven nights and the timber blazed
for more days than most people kept counting.
Even when every magnetic mine
had been located and cleared, there were dangers.
Centuries of waste had silted the river
till the water ran black over Teddington weir
and a bag of rubbish thrown from London Bridge
took six weeks to ride a dying current
out to the estuary. No swimming, no fish,
and those who fell in had to be sluiced out.
No ships, no work. The industry found itself
caught in the net of passing time,
watching mile after mile of dockland fill
with silence and absence. Land changed hands
in an estate agent's office, short-lease premises
with 'Upstream' and 'Downstream' carved above the doors.
Now the tidal traffic is a slow weekday flow of cars
channeled into streets built before cars were thought of.
They inch round corners, nudge against kerbs,
then settle tight packed against the pavement.
On Butler's Wharf, the only machinery
now in daily use is the tow-away truck:
cruising yellow lines, it pauses to hoist
the solid engineering of a badly parked BMW
into the air with illogical ease.

In Coriander Building, an agency
maintains the plants, the colour scheme is neutral
but the smell of new paint has yet to sink in,
like the spice that still seasons the air after rain.
A film crew arrives, on a costly location shoot
for *Jack the Ripper*. It's a crowded night.
Intent on atmosphere, they've cluttered the alleys
with urchins, trollops and guttersnipes
who drift to the waterfront when they're not working
and gaze across at the biggest, emptiest office block in Europe
and its undefendable, passing light.

Lavinia Greenlaw

The River Idle

Here the River Idle sidles leisurely across the plain
Broad between the bending willows; grey beneath the tilting rain,
Like a looking-glass reflecting silent trees and whistling train.

Toyshop-train that rattles seaward, over bridges clattering on
Sometimes by the river, sometimes fields away in miles alone,
Never stopping, never slowing till the clockwork journey's done.

Under bridges running darkly, running on yet not away,
The Idle winds unsleeping Ss through the seasons, green and grey,
Where endings run into beginnings in the round of night and day.

Phoebe Hesketh

River in the Valley

We cross the Sacramento River at Colusa
follow the road on the levee south and east
find thousands of swallows nesting

on the underside of a concrete overhead
roadway? causeway? abandoned. Near
        Butte Creek.

    Gen runs in little circles looking up
    at swoops of swallows—laughing—
        they keep
    flowing under the bridge and out,

    Kai leans silent against a concrete pier
    tries to hold with his eyes the course
    of a single darting bird,

    I pick grass seeds from my socks.

The coast range. Parched yellow front hills,
blue-gray thornbrush higher hills behind.
And here is the Great Central Valley,
drained, then planted and watered,
    thousand-foot deep soils
    thousand-acre orchards

    Sunday morning,
only one place serving breakfast
in Colusa, old river and tractor men
sipping milky coffee.

From north of Sutter Buttes
we see snow on Mt. Lassen
and the clear arc of the Sierra
south to the Desolation peaks.
One boy asks, "where do rivers start?"
in threads in hills, and gather down to here—
but the river
is all of it everywhere,
all flowing at once,
all one place.

                        Gary Snyder

The River Meadows

(In Flood)

LIX

Then, to conclude these pleasant Acts,
Denton sets ope its *Cataracts*;
And makes the Meadow truly be
(What it but seem'd before) a Sea.
For, jealous of its *Lords* long stay,
It try's t'invite him thus away.
The River in it self is drown'd,
And Isles th'astonisht Cattle round.

LX

Let others tell the *Paradox*,
How Eels now bellow in the Ox;
How Horses at their Tails to kick,
Turn'd as they hang to Leeches quick;
How Boats can over Bridges sail;
And Fishes do the Stables scale.
How *Salmons* trespassing are found;
And Pikes are taken in the Pound.

LXI

But I, retiring from the Flood,
Take Sanctuary in the Wood.

Andrew Marvell
from The Lyrics

The River of Rivers in Connecticut

There is a great river this side of Stygia,
Before one comes to the first black cataracts
And trees that lack the intelligence of trees.

In that river, far this side of Stygia,
The mere flowing of the water is a gayety,
Flashing and flashing in the sun. On its banks,

No shadow walks. The river is fateful,
Like the last one. But there is no ferryman.
He could not bend against its propelling force.

It is not to be seen beneath the appearances
That tell of it. The steeple at Farmington
Stands glistening and Haddam shines and sways.

It is the third commonness with light and air,
A curriculum, a vigor, a local abstraction . . .
Call it, once more, a river, an unnamed flowing,

Space-filled, reflecting the seasons, the folk-lore
Of each of the senses, call it, again and again,
The river that flows nowhere, like a sea.

Wallace Stevens

River People

The sandy spurs made desert islands
when the river ran low, its stench
unique and alien to the children,
making their tentative families.
Swans were enemy craft, or merely
swans, but whoever destroyed their young
were not of the river people; these

speculated on the birds
gravely, and left them alone.

They would never find fossils in that gritty
soil, nothing except the recognisable
junk of their own lives cast from the rot:
a boot, a bicycle wheel; but the depths
drew them. Even the meadows, rich
and damp, blazing pollen in every
buttercup, failed to enchant. The children,
in their season, immemorially
crouched by the river to make their lives.

Joan Downar

River Profile
Our body is a moulded river
NOVALIS

Out of a bellicose fore-time, thundering
head-on collisions of cloud and rock in an
up-thrust, crevasse-and-avalanche, troll country,
deadly to breathers,

it whelms into our picture below the melt-line,
where tarns lie frore under frowning cirques, goat-bell,
wind-breaker, fishing-rod, miner's-lamp country,
already at ease with

the mien and gestures that become its kindness,
in streams, still anonymous, still jumpable,
flows as it should through any declining country
in probing spirals.

Soon of a size to be named and the cause of
dirty in-fighting among rival agencies,

down a steep stair, penstock-and-turbine country,
it plunges ram-stam,

to foam through a wriggling gorge incised in softer
strata, hemmed between crags that nauntle heaven,
robber-baron, tow-rope, portage-way country,
nightmare of merchants.

Disemboguing from foothills, now in hushed meanders,
now in riffling braids, it vaunts across a senile
plain, well-entered, chateau-and-cider-press country,
its regal progress

gallanted for a while by quibbling poplars,
then by chimneys: led off to cool and launder
retort, steam-hammer, gasometer country,
it changes color.

Polluted, bridged by girders, banked by concrete,
now it bisects a polyglot metropolis,
ticker-tape, taxi, brothel, foot-lights country,
à-la-mode always.

Broadening or burrowing to the moon's phases,
turbid with pulverised wastemantle, on through
flatter, duller, hotter, cotton-gin country
it scours, approaching

the tidal mark where it puts off majesty,
disintegrates, and through swamps of a delta,
punting-pole, fowling-piece, oyster-tongs country,
wearies to its final

act of surrender, effacement, atonement
in a huge amorphous aggregate no cuddled
attractive child ever dreams of, non-country,
image of death as

a spherical dew-drop of life. Unlovely
monsters, our tales believe, can be translated
too, even as water, the selfless mother
of all especials.

W. H. Auden

River rising in India

A man sits fishing on the sultry bank
Of the great river. Nothing stirs except
The earth cracking under the sleepless sun
And fish that lie embedded in the mud.

Looking up once he sees the wall of water—
Hardly believes its power, but if he had known
Could have done nothing. The mile of fields to his village,
Weary to trudge at evening, and all the houses
And many villages and the whole valley
Is drowned in half an hour.

We in a quieter land may sense the rise
Of other rivers, gathering at the source
The wherewithal to ruin us. At heart
We can do nothing beyond watch it come.

In India they cannot mourn their dead
They are too many, and an aeroplane
Viewing the scene notices only sun
Polishing water stretching in its right:
None of the wreckage shows. Why should we then
Lament the imminent surrender of
One among thousand hearts swept beyond hearing?

Jenny Joseph

River Song

Summer is draining away, and you, swift running
River—River, carry our songs away,
Over your shifting mirrors, to the cavernous-rooted
Alders leaning low where you swirl complaining.

You who have known the swan and the paddling mallard
And a long grimy day grim barges toiling,
And sweep at last to a tangle of insane wharves,
Talkative river—carry our songs away.

You who have echoed the lute, borne gilded barges,
You who have been polluted, but feel no pain—
Sound to our sunlight songs, you elemental;
You will not hear them again, hear them again.

John Heath-Stubbs

'The Riverbed . . .'
for Bernard and Jane McCabe

The riverbed, dried-up, half-full of leaves.

Us, listening to a river in the trees.

Seamus Heaney
from The Haw Lantern *(1987)*

Riverine

for Jim Reed

'. . . weil Glückseligkeit nicht ein Ideal
der Vernunft, sondern der Einbildung ist.'

Kant.

Above the fall, of course, nothing is declined,
All gestures repeat an infinite concordance
In ranks of matching trees, each phase of moon,
The regular dimpling rain, whose liquid pebbles
Will always fall plumb dead centre, rippling out
And out in regular encores. Here, any number
Of silent kings might come and go, their beards
Miraculously still among rhythmic rowers;
Or ladies proffer or retrieve as many swords
As you like; or pale girls loosely wrapped in white
Drift smiling by, immersed in death's long dreaming.

Only at the lip, as the water silkily pours
And tips, does the river find time and tense, the lively
Rage of moment, in which the unbottled torrent
Wells forward and down in plaited layer on layer
Of contradiction, wording into a love
Crazy with twists and turns and sudden pleas—
Too much always said, and always at too great length.
Yet what could be more reasonable than gravity?
And nothing dazzles more than the splinters thrown
Up from rocks, or shines more deeply than the coils
Of pools, or refreshes more from two meadows off.

Downstream, the estuary exhales, its broad banks
Smacking of salt. What were those distant chasms
Reeking of poet's garlic, those sleek distances
Higher than bluebell woods, except a long-ago
Love affair well within range of eloquence?
But the silver fish that thuds upstream risks even
The rosiest of its precious blood to haul

Its bursting muscle of self, that intent eye,
Back through the roaring foam to that calm notion
Where, unbroken, the waters of the womb still mull
All the unspoken possible words of happiness.

Lawrence Sail

Rivers
(The Thames, August–November 1973)

1.

The sky dark blue, the sun a butter-pat:
confusion of dark leaf, harvest machines
the shaking and the rattling and the dust.
This small river should grow a new skin.
I wish well to the fish.
I have had this face for forty-two years:
no partridges or hares are in my grain,
then I should grow a sort of river-skin
and glitter and die like a sun-fragment.
Sullen continuation of dark leaf
daubing the moon's road blotching the sun's:
a stronger smell than the dust
a sharper smell than the mist,
living by the confusion of dark leaf.

2.

Diving off a road-bridge a young gnat
three seconds in mid-air.
Sunny brick, river so old and green
there might be no upstream,
and is there any pure source to swim in?
I am a tree-head in its own shadow.
Rivers are for upstream.
Long time is for walking beside them.

Or be a bird with crimson at the breast
swoops in what time has eaten running back.
I meditate the sun, his energies,
always walk in the straggle of his rays.

3.

Come along brain-bone, come and see
this curdled river under sparks of rain
as lucid as a bream ignite himself,
ruffle his bank and run black under it.
Come and climb up into a tree.
Willows with ashes brush together.
The air's electric, heaven is pregnant
but time is slow, the season is slow.
Consider your future O mankind:
only the swans will need no shelter,
they shake their feathers and they die.
I need a shelter. We need a shelter.
The globe is never still.

4.

Scruffy meadows endless by the railway,
then walking in the wet and shaggy grass
you might plunge your head in the cool sun
and keep on walking. Oh to be still.
Oh sober drunkenness. Yellow light.
The season tilting and the hour tilting.
An animal speaking in a meadow
heavenly mysteries running like rivers
has planted a black shadow on the green.

5.

Now we are worse than then.
The blighted summer like a throat:
I drink the diseases of London.
You would be silent at such a time,

the chemist has no remedy for love.
A river maintaining a small language,
the monologues of reason,
moss, pebble, autumn flower:
the solitude the river created:
In my head I am walking in it
light as a hare, we are like hares in grass,
and we behave as they do in autumn.

6.

It drizzled.
The air is full of leaves and drizzle.
The lamplight is small in the empty road.
Waking at dawn, who I am, where I am.
Once when the lamplighter passed at five
brushing the skin of the wet hedge
the streetlight had long rays like crocodiles.
Much later in the dawn anonymous
the swishing taxis the suburban birds
waking at dawn smelling like a small town.
Oh to be in love in eighteen eighty.
Oh to be at peace in nineteen ten.
I want the future of mankind.
I copy out the music of the people.
Léger painted the bones of the new world.
I write your name.

7.

Indoors the images of the Virgin,
doe-eyed mercy, faces from the kitchen.
Moral machines are never in control.
My life has been entangled in a tree,
the dust of books, a cat, the betting-shop,
the stone inside what is alive,
breathing paint-fumes, coughing coal-dust.
It is soon black enough to have courage,

and conversation is black and cold.
There is nowhere except through the leaves,
the rain hangs in the darkening air.

8.

A limestone statue in a meadow
cut off by railings is father Thames,
the steady local trickle of his springs
continues like starlight.
Shall be my father and my grandfather.
Trees are the pyramids and spires of light,
they are a coarseness in the mind of God,
he dribbles a streaky-coloured mist
between the greying bodies of the trees.
Is tough enough to talk in English.
The leaves are turning high on every hill.

9.

Early winter. It is wet in the field.
There is something discarded about mist.
I like this hush,
ditches of black enamel, motionless dead leaf,
pink in the dawn's cheek,
the ice-axes of light hammer stone.
River-water is moral but obscure.
There is no edge of nature.
There are no contrivances left in the world.
I like to see these robust colours.

Peter Levi

'Rivers arise; whether thou be the Son'

Rivers arise; whether thou be the Son
Of utmost *Tweed*, or *Oose*, or gulphie *Dun*,
Or *Trent*, who like some earth-born Giant spreads
His thirty Armes along the indented Meads,
Or sullen *Mole* that runneth underneath,
Or *Severn* swift, guilty of Maidens death,
Or Rockie *Avon*, or of Sedgie *Lee*,
Or Coaly *Tine*, or ancient hallowd *Dee*,
Or *Humber* loud that keeps the *Scythians* Name,
Or *Medway* smooth, or Royal Towred *Thame*.

John Milton
from 'At a Vacation Exercise in the College'

'The river's tent is broken: the last fingers of leaf'

The river's tent is broken: the last fingers of leaf
Clutch and sink into the wet bank. The wind
Crosses the brown land, unheard. The nymphs are departed.
Sweet Thames, run softly, till I end my song.
The river bears no empty bottles, sandwich papers,
Silk handkerchiefs, cardboard boxes, cigarette ends
Or other testimony of summer nights. The nymphs are departed.
And their friends, the loitering heirs of city directors;
Departed, have left no addresses.
By the waters of Leman I sat down and wept . . .
Sweet Thames, run softly till I end my song,
Sweet Thames, run softly, for I speak not loud or long.

T. S. Eliot
from 'The Fire Sermon', The Waste Land

Riverside

In this river-side town
The side-streets narrow to a view
Of water flowing as if across a frame,
A greenish brown
Almost unnoticed, just a band
At motion passing through
Groups of grey buildings, and the same
Grey-colour opposite, across flat land;

Until the angled line
Of a ship's bow slides
Across the picture like a wedge
Furrowing the river and pushing the two sides
Further apart by the surprise,
Which draws me down to the water's edge:
As if this were a sign,
And I couldn't believe my eyes.

Then listening, watching, as part
Of the beyond of the picture I stand;
And the ships go by.
At times the potential of the sight
Is desire, a tang of mud in the estuary;
Or the composition is an art
Of meditation, a composure of dry land.
Finally, at night,

When power-station stacks are lit
With rows of lamps, and up-river the twin
Giant pylons hang like Christmas trees,
And navigation colours fall
Across the water, all there is to see
Are hints of what composes it
Now that the picture's dark. Then I begin
To gather it home and settle it on the wall,

Part of the well-known at last.
Along the main streets,
Rarely disturbed by weather
Or driven by the sea, dawdling in shops
We dwindle towards home together
With what we have fixed upon: and what completes
Our going, like an instinct, like a taste,
Turns below thought, and never stops.

Michael Vince

Round Oak and Eastwell

In my own native field two fountains run
All desolate and naked to the sun;
The fell destroyer's hand hath reft their side
Of every tree that hid and beautified
Their shallow waters in delightful clumps,
That sunburnt now o'er pebbles skips and jumps.
One where stone quarries in its hills are broke
Still keeps its ancient pastoral name, Round Oak,
Although one little solitary tree
Is all that's left of its old pedigree;
The other, more deformed, creeps down the dell,
Scarcely the shade of what was once Eastwell,
While the elm-groves that groaned beneath no tax
Have paid their tribute to the lawless axe,
And the old rooks that waited other springs
Have fled to stranger scenes on startled wings.
The place all lonely and all naked lies,
And Eastwell spring in change's symphonies
Boils up its sand unnoticed and alone,
To all its former happiness unknown,
Its glory gone, its Sunday pastimes o'er,
The haunts of shepherds and of maids no more.

The passer-by unheeding tramples on
Nor heeds the spring, nor trees nor bushes gone,
While the stray poet's memory haunts the spot
Like a friend's features time hath nigh forgot.

John Clare

Ruskin Remembered

What is it tunes a Scottish stream so fine?
Concurrence of the rock and of the rain.
Much rain must fall, and yet not of a sort
That tears the hills down, carries them off in sport.
The rocks must break irregularly, jagged—
Our Yorkshire shales, carpenter-like, form merely
Tables and shelves for rain to drip and leap
Down from; the rocks of Cumberland and Wales
Are of too bold a cut and so keep back
Those chords their streams should multiply and mingle.
But there must be hard pebbles too—within
The loosely breaking rock, to strew a shingle
Along the level shore—white, for the brown
Water in rippling threads to wander through
In amber gradations to the brink, the ear
Filled with the link on link of travelling sound,
Like heard divisions, crisp above a ground,
Defining a contentment that suffices—
As walking to unblent music, such as this.

Charles Tomlinson

Rustic Fishing

On Sunday mornings, freed from hard employ,
How oft I mark the mischievous young boy
With anxious haste his pole and lines provide,
For makeshifts oft crook'd pins to thread were tied;
And delve his knife with wishes ever warm
In rotten dunghills for the grub and worm,
The harmless treachery of his hooks to bait;
Tracking the dewy grass with many a mate,
To seek the brook that down the meadows glides,
Where the grey willow shadows by its sides,
Where flag and reed in wild disorder spread,
And bending bulrush bows its taper head;
And, just above the surface of the floods,
Where water-lilies mount their snowy buds,
On whose broad swimming leaves of glossy green
The shining dragon-fly is often seen;
Where hanging thorns, with roots wash'd bare, appear,
That shield the moor-hen's nest from year to year;
While crowding osiers mingling wild among
Prove snug asylums to her brood when young,
Who, when surpris'd by foes approaching near,
Plunge 'neath the weeping boughs and disappear.
There far from terrors that the parson brings,
Or church bell hearing when its summons rings,
Half hid in meadow-sweet and keck's high flowers,
In lonely sport they spend the Sunday hours.
Though ill supplied for fishing seems the brook,
That breaks the mead in many a stinted crook,
Oft chok'd in weeds, and foil'd to find a road,
The choice retirement of the snake and toad,
Then lost in shallows dimpling restlessly,
In fluttering struggles murmuring to be free—
O'er gravel stones its depth can scarcely hide
It runs the remnant of its broken tide,
Till, seemly weary of each chok'd control,
It rests collected in some gulled hole

Scoop'd by the sudden floods when winter's snow
Melts in confusion by a hasty thaw;
There bent in hopeful musings on the brink
They watch their floating corks that seldom sink,
Save when a wary roach or silver bream
Nibbles the worm as passing up the stream,
Just urging expectation's hopes to stay
To view the dodging cork, then slink away;
Still hopes keep burning with untir'd delight,
Still wobbling curves keep wavering like a bite:
If but the breezy wind their floats should spring,
And move the water with a troubling ring,
A captive fish still fills the anxious eyes
And willow-wicks lie ready for the prize;
Till evening gales awaken damp and chill,
And nip the hopes that morning suns instil,
And resting flies have tired their gauzy wing,
Nor longer tempt the watching fish to spring,
Who at the worm no nibbles more repeat,
But lunge from night in sheltering flag-retreat.
Then disappointed in their day's employ,
They seek amusement in a feebler joy.
Short is the sigh for fancies prov'd untrue:
With humbler hopes still pleasure they pursue
Where the rude oak-bridge scales the narrow pass,
Half hid in rustling reeds and scrambling grass,
Or stepping-stones stride o'er the narrow sloughs
Which maidens daily cross to milk their cows;
There they in artless glee for minnows run,
And wade and dabble past the setting sun,
Chasing the struttle o'er the shallow tide,
And flat stones turning up where gudgeons hide.
All former hopes their ill success delay'd,
In this new change they fancy well repaid.
And thus they wade, and chatter o'er their joys
Till night, unlook'd-for, young success destroys,
Drives home the sons of solitude and streams,

And stops uncloy'd hope's ever-fresh'ning dreams.
They then, like schoolboys that at truant play,
In sloomy fear lounge on their homeward way,
And inly tremble, as they gain the town,
Where chastisement awaits with many a frown,
And hazel twigs, in readiness prepar'd,
For their long absence bring a meet reward.

John Clare

St Winefride's Well

Overhead the wren builds
in the ruined mudcup of the swallow
and a stone pilgrim bears another
on his shoulder. I sip at the step
like an animal at a waterhole.

Here water swallows itself
unravelling its knotwork between ice-ages,
as the sea's slippery pages
turning forever
at the edge of the mind.

It flowers with a small sob
on a powerful stem from a tap-root deep
in a broken earth, a pulse
almost flesh, when the scalpel reveals
the drumming loneliness of the heart.

Just to look is healing,
to stand in the porch of summer
and stare through turbulence
into the dark.

Gillian Clarke

Salmon

first for, and now in memory of, Ceri Richards

The river sucks them home.
The lost past claims them.
   Beyond the headland
It gropes into the channel
Of the nameless sea.
   Off-shore they submit
To the cast, to the taste of it.
It releases them from salt,
Their thousand miles in odyssey
For spawning. It rehearsed their return
   From the beginning; now
   It clenches them like a fist.

The echo of once being here
Possesses and inclines them.
   Caught in the embrace
Of nothing that is not now,
Riding in with the tide-race,
   Not by their care,
Not by any will they know,
They turn fast to the caress
Of their only course. Sea-hazards done,
They ache towards the one world
   From which their secret
   Sprang, perpetuate

More than themselves, the ritual
Claim of the river, pointed
   Towards rut, tracing
Their passion out. Weeping philosopher,
They reaffirm the world,
   The stars by which they ran,
Now this precise place holds them
Again. They reach the churning wall

Of the brute waterfall which shed
Them young from its cauldron pool.
  A hundred times
  They lunge and strike

Against the hurdles of the rock;
Though hammering water
  Beats them back
Still their desire will not break.
They flourish, whip and kick,
  Tensile for their truth's
Sake, give to the miracle
Of their treadmill leaping
The illusion of the natural.
The present in torrential flow
  Nurtures its own
  Long undertow:

They work it, strike and streak again,
Filaments in suspense.
  The lost past shoots them
Into flight, out of their element,
In bright transilient sickle-blades
  Of light; until upon
The instant's height of their inheritance
They chance in descant over the loud
Diapasons of flood, jack out of reach
And snatch of clawing water,
  Stretch and soar
  Into easy rapids

Beyond, into half-haven, jounce over
Shelves upstream; and know no question
  But, pressed by their cold blood,
Glance through the known maze.
They unravel the thread to source
  To die at their ancestry's
Last knot, knowing no question.

They meet under hazel trees,
Are chosen, and so mate. In shallows as
The stream slides clear yet shirred
   With broken surface where
   Stones trap the creamy stars

Of air, she scoops at gravel with fine
Thrust of her exact blind tail;
   At last her lust
Gapes in a gush on her stone nest
And his held, squanderous peak
   Shudders his final hunger
On her milk; seed laid on seed
In spunk of liquid silk.
So in exhausted saraband their slack
Convulsions wind and wend galactic
   Seed in seed, a found
   World without end.

The circle's set, proportion
Stands complete, and,
   Ready for death,
Haggard they hang in aftermath
Abundance, ripe for the world's
   Rich night, the spear.
Why does this fasting fish
So haunt me? Gautama, was it this
You saw from river-bank
At Uruvela? Was this
   Your glimpse
   Of holy law?

John Ormond

The Salmon Leap

I saw one shadow shoot up and over
While ten failed to make it again and again,
But most of the salmon without an effort
In the bottom of the pool all day had lain.

Suddenly, effortlessly, like a flight of birds,
Up and over I saw them all slip.
The secret, I think, was the melted snow
Coming down and flicking them like a whip.

The majority of people make no attempt
In life to explore the infinite,
But who can tell what Death's cold touch
May prompt the lazy louts to yet?

Hugh MacDiarmid

Sands of the Well

The golden particles
descend, descend,
traverse the water's
depth and come to rest
on the level bed
of the well until,
the full descent
accomplished, water's
absolute transparence
is complete, unclouded
by constellations
of bright sand.
Is this
the place where you
are brought in meditation?

Transparency
seen for itself—
as if its quality
were not, after all,
to enable
perception *not* of itself?
With a wand
of willow I again
trouble the envisioned pool,
the cloudy nebulae
form and disperse,
the separate
grains again
slowly, slowly
perform their descent,
and again
stillness ensues,
and the mystery
of that sheer
clarity, is it water indeed,
or air, or light?

Denise Levertov

Sap

Where the stream ox-bowed
And we stood on a bulwark
Of planks and turf, the current
Made its darkest passage,
A black stillwater, treacherous
Beneath a sheen of scum.

Once, and only once, a trout rose,
Its lean sides gleaming like
A knife between the stones,
Crimson shadow at its belly.

Yet how often was the only sound
Not the Ffornwg or our
White thrash after fish,
But the thinnest flute of the sap
Maintaining its single note
A long minute in my head
As I imagined that pressure
Of water rising through the trees,
Streams moving vertically
And spilling in a silent turbulence
Along the boughs, a river

Flowing there beneath the bark,
The sap, singing, even as flesh
Leaned white and stunned
Against the visible current,
And the gwrachen like a small
Green stick swam past the hand.

Robert Minhinnick

Scotland in an Oxford Landscape

The stream's tidy banks have fled,
routed, when the river took the borderland
and lost its own identity. Isolated trees
mark mere possibilities, as if this were
a medieval map, where stained brown outlines
suggest the edge of a world which has been
heard of but not yet visited. Dabchicks
drift nodding on the current between,
as though the trunks were supports
for toppled dolmens and they sounded ley lines
like diviners. Beneath, lies debris:
the small river animals' habitats, voles,
otters, rats, avenues of spring anemones,

and tiny wild crocuses that smudge your eyesight
briefly, with enigmatic purple. Treasure,
to be found again, of a more bucolic Atlantis.

Olivia Byard

Severnside

We looked for the tide, for the full river
  Riding up the expanse to the further cliff:
But its bed lay bare—sand
  That a brisk wind planed towards us.
Perpetual shore it seemed, stretch
  And invitation to all we could see and more:
Hard to think of it as a thoroughfare for shoals:
  At the edge, a cracked mosaic of mud,
Even shards of it dried in the sunny wind—
  A wind whose tidal sound mocked tidelessness,
Mocked, too, the grounded barges grass now occupied
  Dense on the silt-filled holds. Sad,
But a glance told you that land had won,
  That we would see no swell today
Impelled off the Atlantic, shelving
  And channelling riverwards in the hour we had.
And so we turned, and the wind possessed our ears,
  Mocked on, and our talk turned, too,
Mind running on future things,
  Null to all save the blind pull of muscle
In a relegated present. When we paused
  The sands were covered and the channels full:
We had attended the wind too long, robbed
  Of distinction between the thing it was
And what it imitated. But the rise we stood on,
  Reawakening our eyes, gave back suddenly
More than the good that we had forfeited:
  Ahead—below—we could sight now

The present, as it were, spread to futurity
  And up the river's bend and bed
The waters travelling, a prow of light
  Pushing the foam before them in its onrush
Over the waiting sand. And we who seemed
  To be surfing forward on that white
Knew that we only dreamed of standing still
  Here where a tide whose coming we had missed
Rode massed before us in the filled divide.

Charles Tomlinson

Shadwell Stair

I am the ghost of Shadwell Stair.
  Along the wharves by the water-house,
  And through the dripping slaughter-house,
I am the shadow that walks there.

Yet I have flesh both firm and cool,
  And eyes tumultuous as the gems
  Of moons and lamps in the lapping Thames
When dusk sails wavering down the pool.

Shuddering the purple street-arc burns
  Where I watch always; from the banks
  Dolorously the shipping clanks,
And after me a strange tide turns.

I walk till the stars of London wane
  And dawn creeps up the Shadwell Stair.
  But when the crowing syrens blare
I with another ghost am lain.

Wilfred Owen

Sibard's Well

My house, named for the Saxon spring,
Stands by the sour farmyard, the long-
Dry lip that once was Sibard's Well
Buried beneath a winding-stone
To stop the cattle falling in;
Yet underfoot is still the sound
At last of night, at first of day,
In country silences, a thin
Language of water through the clay.

At mornings, in small light, I hear
Churn-clink, the bucket handle fall.
An iron shirt, a sudden spear
Unprop themselves from the farm wall.
A voice, in a far, altered speech
Beneath my window seems to say,
'I too lived here. I too awoke
In quarter-light, when life's cold truth
Was all too clear. As clearly spoke.'

Charles Causley

'So went he playing on the watery plaine'

So went he playing on the watery plaine.
  Soone after whom the louely Bridegroome came,
  The noble Thamis, with all his goodly traine,
  But him before there went, as best became,
  His auncient parents, namely th'auncient Thame.
  But much more aged was his wife then he,
  The Ouze, whom men doe Isis rightly name;
  Full weake and crooked creature seemed shee,
And almost blind through eld, that scarce her way could see.

Therefore on either side she was sustained
  Of two smal grooms, which by their names were hight
  The *Churne*, and *Charwell*, two small streames, which pained
  Them selues her footing to direct aright,
  Which fayled oft through faint and feeble plight:
  But *Thame* was stronger, and of better stay;
  Yet seem'd full aged by his outward sight,
  With head all hoary, and his beard all gray,
Deawed with siluer drops, that trickled downe alway.

And eke he somewhat seem'd to stoupe afore
  With bowed backe, by reason of the lode,
  And auncient heauy burden, which he bore
  Of that faire City, wherein make abode
  So many learned impes, that shoote abrode,
  And with their braunches spred all Britany,
  No lesse then do her elder sisters broode.
  Ioy to you both, ye double noursery,
Of Arts, but Oxford thine doth *Thame* most glorify.

Edmund Spenser
from The Faerie Queene

The Soaking

The rain has come, and the earth must be very glad
Of its moisture, and the made roads all dust clad;
It lets a friendly veil down on the lucent dark,
And not of any bright ground thing shows any spark.

Tomorrow's grey morning will show cow-parsley,
Hung all with shining drops, and the river will be
Duller because of all the soddenness of things,
Till the skylark breaks his reluctance, hangs shaking, and sings.

Ivor Gurney

XII Song

Memory, hither come,
  And tune your merry notes;
And, while upon the wind
  Your music floats,
I'll pore upon the stream,
Where sighing lovers dream,
And fish for fancies as they pass
Within the watery glass.

I'll drink of the clear stream,
  And hear the linnet's song;
And there I'll lie and dream
  The day along:
And, when night comes, I'll go
To places fit for woe;
Walking along the darkened valley
With silent melancholy.

William Blake

The Song of the Brook

I come from haunts of coot and hern,
  I make a sudden sally,
And sparkle out among the fern,
  To bicker down a valley.

By thirty hills I hurry down,
  Or slip between the ridges,
By twenty thorps, a little town,
  And half a hundred bridges.

Till last by Philip's farm I flow
  To join the brimming river,
For men may come and men may go,
  But I go on forever.

148

I chatter over stony ways,
  In little sharps and trebles,
I bubble into eddying bays,
  I babble on the pebbles.

With many a curve my banks I fret
  By many a field and fallow,
And many a fairy foreland set
  With willow-weed and mallow.

I chatter, chatter, as I flow
  To join the brimming river,
For men may come and men may go,
  But I go on forever.

I wind about, and in and out,
  With here a blossom sailing,
And here and there a lusty trout,
  And here and there a grayling,

And here and there a foamy flake
  Upon me, as I travel
With many a silvery water-break
  Above the golden gravel,

And draw them all along and flow
  To join the brimming river,
For men may come and men may go,
  But I go on forever.

I steal by lawns and grassy plots,
  I slide by hazel covers;
I move the sweet forget-me-nots
  That grow for happy lovers.

I slip, I slide, I gloom, I glance,
  Among my skimming swallows;
I make the netted sunbeam dance
  Against my sandy shallows.

I murmur under moon and stars
  In brambly wildernesses;
I linger by my shingly bars,
  I loiter round my cresses;

And out again I curve and flow
  To join the brimming river,
For men may come and men may go,
  But I go on forever.

Alfred, Lord Tennyson

Sonnet

Jordan that feeds from far Mount Hermon's snow,
Thames with its fogs and warehouses and docks,
Dargle whose alders dip on little rocks,
The Nile where heavily feluccas go,
Untroubled Avon in flat watermeadow
Or the mad pacing Rhine of many shocks,
Medway that swings the tackle through the blocks,
Deben now still, but for two boys who row;
The waters that will storm a city's gate
Or lie in glazing pools above a slope,
Or lessen, or become immoderate:
All these I feel within me and their scope
Carried by veins throughout my whole estate,
So quiet is my face and wild my hope.

Sheila Wingfield

Dargle: a source of the River Liffey

Sonnet to the River Otter

Dear native brook! wild streamlet of the West!
  How many various-fated years have past,
   What happy, and what mournful hours, since last
I skimmed the smooth thin stone along thy breast,
Numbering its light leaps! yet so deep imprest
Sink the sweet scenes of childhood, that mine eyes
  I never shut amid the sunny ray,
But straight with all their tints thy waters rise,
  Thy crossing plank, thy marge with willows grey,
And bedded sand that, veined with various dyes,
Gleamed through thy bright transparence! On my way,
  Visions of childhood! oft have ye beguiled
Lone manhood's cares, yet waking fondest sighs:
Ah! that once more I were a careless child!

Samuel Taylor Coleridge

The Spring at Chedworth

There is no goddess in the spring
the sturdy walls are bare.
The painted plaster crumbled
colours danced into the air.
The Victorian explorers
found their nymph no longer there.

She would not wait to greet them
though her mouth was never still.
Her baths, where girls sat idly
they miscalled a fulling mill.
'Nymphaeum' fades their labels
where the empty waters spill.

I have seen her in the August yard,
shriek, beneath the hose,
leap in a Welsh river
in her rough and sweat-streaked clothes.
But desire runs through her fingers
she is gone as water goes.

She left inside her basin
a black beetle which clasps tight
a bead of air, her glistening gift,
as he spirals, out of sight,
as the cuckoo in the wet trees
as her laughter in the night.

Alison Brackenbury

Spring Tide

I

I seem lower than the distant waves,
Their roar diluting to the stillness
Of the sea's progression across these flats,
A map of water so adjusted
It behaves like a preservative
And erases neither the cattle's
And the sheep's nor my own footprints.
I leave hieroglyphics under glass
As well as feathers that hardly budge,
Down abandoned at preening places
That last so long as grassy islands
Where swans unravel among the ferns.

II

It isn't really a burial mound
Reflected there, but all that remains
Of a sandy meadow, a graveyard

Where it was easy to dig the graves.
The spring tide circles and excavates
A shrunken ramshackle pyramid
Rinsing cleaner scapulae, tibias,
Loose teeth, cowrie and nautilus shells
Before seeping after sun and moon
To pour cupfuls into the larks' nests,
To break a mirror on the grazing
And lift minnows over the low bridge.

III

The spring tide has ferried jelly fish
To the end of the lane, pinks, purples,
Wet flowers beside the floating cow-pats.
The zig-zags I make take me among
White cresses and brookweed, lousewort,
Water plantain and grass of parnassus
With engraved capillaries, ivory sheen:
By a dry-stone wall in the dune slack
The greenish sepals, the hidden blush
And a lip's red veins and yellow spots—
Marsh helleborine waiting for me
To come and go with the spring tide.

Michael Longley

Springhead at Fontmell Magna

Music within the green and rounded hill,
A gift of the chalk,
Downland that bubbles to the surface
A small white symphony of clear water,
Pure and without distraction,
Each note, a silver messenger
Glistening in the sun light,
A miracle that you can dip your hand into.

And once you have tasted that music
You return again and again
To hear the echo running downstream,
Fleet of foot, its innocence engraved on your heart,
Beneath the roots of trees,
A sacred welling up, a hidden purpose
A place of pilgrimage and offering,
A prayer that is answered, and never runs dry.

In memory of Ann Hodgson, Shepherdess.
Ashmore and Fontmell Magna
Who first showed me the spring.
And grazed the sheep on the lynchets above.

James Crowden

Springs
for Ted Hughes

Dying, the salmon
heaves up its head
in the millstream.
Great sores ring
its gills, its eyes,
a burning rust
slowly corrodes
the redgold skin.

Great river king,
nearby the Nore pours
over foaming weirs
its light and music,
endlessly dissolving
walls into webs of
water that drift away
among slow meadows.

But you are abdicating,
you are yielding,
no fight left but in
the hinge of your jaws,
(the hook or *kype*)
gasping, clasping
for a last breath
of this soiled kingdom.

Prince of ocean, from
what shared springs
we pay you homage
we have long forgotten
but I mourn your passing
and would erase
from this cluttered earth
our foul disgrace:

Drain the poison
from the streams,
cleanse the enormous
belly of ocean, tear
those invisible miles
of mesh so that your
kin may course again
through clear waters.

John Montague

The Springs

In a country without saints or shrines
I knew one who made his pilgrimage
to springs, where in his life's dry years
his mind held on. Everlasting,
people call them, and gave them names.
The water broke into sounds and shinings

at the vein mouth, bearing the taste
of the place, the deep rock, sweetness
out of the dark. He bent and drank
in bondage to the ground.

                                    Wendell Berry

The Stream

Pouring of water through the night, through the year,
The last sound before sleep, the first on waking;

Transparent path, almost overgrown beside
The trodden path's embankment of earth and stone;

Clear-bodied wholeness at the field's edge, logic
Finding out the lowest place, the easiest way;

An elemental beside a human sense,
Where he kneels to drink, to paint his skin with cold.

                                    Robert Wells

Sweet Thames Flow Softly

I met my girl at Woolwich Pier, beneath a big crane standing,
And, Oh, the love I felt for her it passed all understanding.
    Took her sailing on the river,
        flow, sweet river, flow,
    London Town was mine to give her,
        sweet Thames flow softly.
    Made the Thames into a crown,
        flow, sweet river, flow,
    Made a brooch of Silvertown,
        sweet Thames flow softly.

At London Yard I held her hand, at Blackwall Point I faced her,
At the Isle of Dogs I kissed her mouth and tenderly embraced her.
    Heard the bells of Greenwich ringing,
        flow, sweet river, flow,
    All the time my heart was singing,
        sweet Thames flow softly.
    Limehouse Reach I gave her there,
        flow, sweet river, flow,
    As a ribbon for her hair,
        sweet Thames flow softly.

From Shadwell Dock to Nine Elms Reach we cheek to cheek were
    dancing,
Her necklace, made of London Bridge, her beauty was enhancing.
    Kissed her once again at Wapping,
        flow, sweet river, flow,
    After that there was no stopping,
        sweet Thames flow softly.
    Richmond Park it was her ring,
        flow, sweet river, flow,
    I'd have given her anything,
        sweet Thames flow softly.

From Rotherhithe to Putney Bridge my love I was declaring,
And she, from Kew to Isleworth, her love to me was swearing.
    Love had set my heart a-burning,
        flow, sweet river, flow,
    Never saw the tide was turning,
        sweet Thames flow softly.
    Gave her Hampton Court to twist,
        flow, sweet river, flow,
    Into a bracelet for her wrist,
        sweet Thames flow softly.

Now, alas, the tide has changed, my love she has gone from me,
And winter's frost has touched my heart and put a blight upon me.
    Creeping fog is on the river,
        flow, sweet river, flow,
    Sun and moon and stars gone with her,
        sweet Thames flow softly.

Swift the Thames runs to the sea,
   flow, sweet river, flow,
Bearing ships and part of me,
   sweet Thames flow softly.

Ewan MacColl

Symphony in Yellow

An omnibus across the bridge
   Crawls like a yellow butterfly,
   And, here and there, a passer-by
Shows like a little restless midge.

Big barges full of yellow hay
   Are moored against the shadowy wharf,
   And, like a yellow silken scarf,
The thick fog hangs along the quay.

The yellow leaves begin to fade
   And flutter from the Temple elms,
   And at my feet the pale green Thames
Lies like a rod of rippled jade.

Oscar Wilde

Tay Bridge

A sky that tastes of rain that's still to fall
And then of rain that falls and tastes of sky . . .
The colour of the country's moist and subtle
In dusk's expected rumour. Amplify
All you can see this evening and the broad
Water enlarges, Dundee slips by an age

Into its land before the lights come on.
Pale, mystic lamps lean on the river-road
Bleaching the city's lunar after-image,
And there's the moon, and there's the setting sun.

The rail bridge melts in a dramatic haze.
Slow visibility—a long train floats
Through a stopped shower's narrow waterways
Above rose-coloured river, dappled motes
In the eye and the narrow piers half-real
Until a cloud somewhere far in the west
Mixes its inks and draws iron and stone
In epic outlines, black and literal.
Now it is simple, weathered, plain, immodest
In waterlight and late hill-hidden sun.

High water adds freshwater-filtered salt
To the aquatic mirrors, a thin spice
That sharpens light on Middle Bank, a lilt
In the reflected moon's analysis.
Mud's sieved and drained from pewter into gold.
Conjectural infinity's outdone
By engineering, light and hydrous fact,
A waterfront that rises fold by fold
Into the stars beyond the last of stone,
A city's elements, local, exact.

Douglas Dunn

Team Gut

I

Who goes there? A scrap-yard river,
A brick-end, drowned-rat, rotten-wharfed river.

Where are you heading? Into the future,
Jiggering out the wastes of labour.

What do you carry? A shaft of nature,
Snaking its way through the neighbourhood factories.

Who are your allies? The dark starlings
That blacken the sky like iron filings

Over smoke-stacks, gasometers, viaducts, tangles
Of rust-speckled dock leaves, and barbed-wire brambles.

Filthy old gut, what plagues do you spread
Through these derelict works? I am memory's thread.

How will you mend them? With hawthorn and rosehips
And fireweed, that burns and peels on the slag-heaps.

II

What do you remember?
Far upstream,
Quiet fields of grass instead of factories,
Sedge turning green.

What more do you remember?
Before the Tyne took shape
I was a mighty river. Glaciers cracked me,
Grinding me deep.

What else do you remember?
Viking raids.
Men who arrived from nowhere, plundered, ruined,
Then sailed away.

Is there more that you remember?
Not long past,
Young lads mined my valley. Some were buried.
I remember dust.

What more can you remember?
Heat and flame,
The fire that buckles rock by the millennium; men
Who briefly did the same.

What burned, do you remember?
Bricks, glass, coke,
And pig-iron, white-hot from the furnace.
A cacophony of smoke.

What's left, now, to remember?
Poisons, the debt
Beneath the smooth, green lawns and tower-blocks.
People forget.

III

What does your name mean, River Team?
To empty and give birth,
To mother, as water always has,
The billion-year-old earth.

Then, River Team, what are men?
No more than coal.
All life on earth is fuel for change.
Men are scarcely a moment old.

But, River Team, what of their works—
Speech, society?
As men forget, so each hurts each,
And all hurt me.

And what is forgetting, River Team?
Only the water
That colours all worn things thrown into it drab
As wormwood in winter.

And what is remembering, River Team?
No single water drop
That circles from sea, by cloud and land, to sea
Is ever lost.

And nothing that time or men can kill,
Or spoil, or change,
Is ever forgotten; for the stream
Of memory remains.

Then what can you know of the grief of men
And women trapped in time?
Only their bodies are water, mostly,
Moving, like mine.

Katrina Porteous

Thames

Good river, it carries
Food for men, for gulls.

Beautiful river
This winter evening
It melts into mauves and greys
Tower, chimney, wharf,
A mirror breathed upon
By haze and the lips of lovers.

This afternoon I saw
My friend's face, purple
After forty days of drifting
Between cold banks, in the brown water;

And drove home, along
The Embankment where he

Had breathed, loitered, loved
In a haze, mauves and greys
While the refuse of gulls, of men
Slapped the black bulk of barges.

White-faced, but with fuel enough,
With food enough to keep going
Today, tomorrow not far from the river,
Still able at times to be fooled,

Down through the rippled lamplight
I drive, into real mud.

Michael Hamburger

The Thames

Thames, the most lov'd of all the Oceans sons,
By his old Sire to his embraces runs,
Hasting to pay his tribute to the Sea,
Like mortal life to meet Eternity.
Though with those streams he no resemblance hold,
Whose foam is Amber, and their Gravel Gold;
His genuine, and less guilty wealth t'explore,
Search not his bottom, but survey his shore;
Ore which he kindly spreads his spacious wing,
And hatches plenty for th'ensuing Spring.
Nor then destroys it with too fond a stay,
Like Mothers which their Infants overlay.
Nor with a sudden and impetuous wave,
Like profuse Kings, resumes the wealth he gave.
No unexpected inundations spoyl
The mowers hopes, nor mock the plowmans toyl:
But God-like his unwearied Bounty flows;
First loves to do, then loves the Good he does.
Nor are his Blessings to his banks confin'd,
But free, and common, as the Sea or Wind;

When he to boast, or to disperse his stores
Full of the tribute of his grateful shores,
Visits the world, and in his flying towers
Brings home to us, and makes both *Indies* ours;
Finds wealth where 'tis, bestows it where it wants
Cities in deserts, wood in Cities plants.
So that to us no thing, no place is strange,
While his fair bosom is the worlds exchange.
O could I flow like thee, and make thy stream
My great example, as it is my theme!
Though deep, yet clear, though gentle, yet not dull,
Strong without rage, without ore-flowing full.

Sir John Denham

'There are too many waterfalls here . . .'

There are too many waterfalls here; the crowded streams
hurry too rapidly down to the sea,
and the pressure of so many clouds on the mountaintops
makes them spill over the sides in soft slow-motion,
turning to waterfalls under our very eyes.
—For if those streaks, those mile-long, shiny, tearstains,
aren't waterfalls yet,
in a quick age or so, as ages go here,
they probably will be.
But if the streams and clouds keep travelling, travelling,
the mountains look like the hulls of capsized ships,
slime-hung and barnacled.

Elizabeth Bishop
From Questions of Travel

'There is a willow grows aslant a brook'

There is a willow grows aslant a brook,
That shows his hoar leaves in the glassy stream;
There with fantastic garlands did she come
Of crow-flowers, nettles, daisies, and long purples
That liberal shepherds give a grosser name,
But our cold maids do dead men's fingers call them:
There, on the pendent boughs her coronet weeds
Clambering to hang, an envious sliver broke;
When down her weedy trophies and herself
Fell in the weeping brook. Her clothes spread wide;
And, mermaid-like, awhile they bore her up:
Which time she chanted snatches of old tunes;
As one incapable of her own distress,
Or like a creature native and indu'd
Unto that element: but long it could not be
Till that her garments, heavy with their drink,
Pull'd the poor wretch from her melodious lay
To muddy death.

William Shakespeare
from Hamlet, *Act 4 Scene 7*

The Third Thing

Water is H_2O, hydrogen two parts, oxygen one,
but there is also a third thing, that makes it water
and nobody knows what that is.

The atom locks up two energies
but it is a third thing present which makes it an atom.

D. H. Lawrence

To my Mistris sitting by a Rivers side
An Eddy

Marke how yond Eddy steales away,
From the rude streame into the Bay,
There lockt up safe, she doth divorce
Her waters from the chanels course,
And scornes the Torrent, that did bring
Her headlong from her native spring.
Now doth she with her new love play,
Whilst he runs murmuring away.
Marke how she courts the bankes, whilst they
As amorously their armes display,
T'embrace, and clip her silver waves:
See how she strokes their sides, and craves
An entrance there, which they deny;
Whereat she frownes, threatning to flye
Home to her streame, and 'gins to swim
Backward, but from the chanels brim,
Smiling, returnes into the creeke,
With thousand dimples on her cheeke.
  Be thou this Eddy, and I'le make
My breast thy shore, where thou shalt take
Secure repose, and never dreame
Of the quite forsaken streame:
Let him to the wide Ocean hast,
There lose his colour, name, and tast;
Thou shalt save all, and safe from him,
Within these armes for ever swim.

Thomas Carew

To the River Charles

River! that in silence windest
    Through the meadows, bright and free,
Till at length thy rest thou findest
    In the bosom of the sea!

Four long years of mingled feeling,
    Half in rest, and half in strife,
I have seen thy waters stealing
    Onward, like the stream of life.

Thou hast taught me, Silent River!
    Many a lesson, deep and long;
Thou hast been a generous giver;
    I can give thee but a song.

Oft in sadness and in illness,
    I have watched thy current glide,
Till the beauty of its stillness
    Overflowed me, like a tide,

And in better hours and brighter,
    When I saw thy waters gleam,
I have felt my heart beat lighter,
    And leap onward with thy stream.

Not for this alone I love thee,
    Nor because thy waves of blue
From celestial seas above thee
    Take their own celestial hue.

Where yon shadowy woodlands hide thee,
    And thy waters disappear,
Friends I love have dwelt beside thee,
    And have made thy margin dear.

More than this;—thy name reminds me
    Of three friends, all true and tried;
And that name, like magic, binds me
    Closer, closer to thy side.

Friends my soul with joy remembers!
    How like quivering flames they start,
When I fan the living embers
    On the hearth-stone of my heart!

'Tis for this, thou Silent River!
    That my spirit leans to thee;
Thou hast been a generous giver
    Take this idle song from me.

H. W. Longfellow

To the River Duddon

I wonder, Duddon, if you still remember
An oldish man with a nose like a pony's nose,
Broad bones, legs long and lean but strong enough
To carry him over Hard Knott at seventy years of age.
He came to you first as a boy with a fishing-rod
And a hunk of Ann Tyson's bread and cheese in his pocket,
Walking from Hawkshead across Walna Scar;
Then as a middle-aged Rydal landlord,
With a doting sister and a government sinecure,
Who left his verses gummed to your rocks like lichen,
The dry and yellow edges of a once-green spring.
He made a guide-book for you, from your source
There where you bubble through the moss on Wrynose
(Among the ribs of bald and bony fells
With screes scratched in the turf like grey scabs),
And twist and slither under humpbacked bridges—
Built like a child's house from odds and ends
Of stones that lie about the mountain side—

Past Cockley Beck Farm and on to Birk's Bridge,
Where the rocks stride about like legs in armour,
And the steel birches buckle and bounce in the wind
With a crinkle of silver foil in the crisp of the leaves;
On then to Seathwaite, where like a steam-navvy
You shovel and slash your way through the gorge
By Wallabarrow Crag, broader now
From becks that flow out of black upland tarns
Or ooze through golden saxifrage and the roots of rowans;
Next Ulpha, where a stone dropped from the bridge
Swims like a tadpole down thirty feet of water
Between steep skirting-boards of rock; and thence
You dribble into lower Dunnerdale
Through wet woods and wood-soil and woodland flowers,
Tutson, the St John's-wort with a single yellow bead,
Marsh marigold, creeping jenny and daffodils;
Here from hazel islands in the late spring
The catkins fall and ride along the stream
Like little yellow weasels, and the soil is loosed
From bulbs of the white lily that smells of garlic,
And dippers rock up and down on rubber legs,
And long-tailed tits are flung through the air like darts;
By Foxfield now you taste the salt in your mouth,
And thrift mingles with the turf, and the heron stands
Watching the wagtails. Wordsworth wrote:
'Remote from every taint of sordid industry'.
But you and I know better, Duddon.
For I, who've lived for nearly thirty years
Upon your shore, have seen the slagbanks slant
Like screes into the sand, and watched the tide
Purple with ore back up the muddy gullies,
And wiped the sinter dust from the farmyard damsons.
A hundred years of floods and rain and wind
Have washed your rocks clear of his words again,
Many of them half-forgotten, brimming the Irish Sea,
But that which Wordsworth knew, even the old man
When poetry had failed like desire, was something
I have yet to learn, and you, Duddon,
Have learned and re-learned to forget and forget again.

Not the radical, the poet and heretic,
To whom the water-forces shouted and the fells
Were like a blackboard for the scrawls of God,
But the old man, inarticulate and humble,
Knew that eternity flows in a mountain beck—
The long cord of the water, the shepherd's numerals
That run upstream, through the singing decades of dialect.
He knew, beneath mutation of year and season,
Flood and drought, frost and fire and thunder,
The blossom on the rowan and the reddening of the berries,
There stands the base and root of the living rock,
Thirty thousand feet of solid Cumberland.

Norman Nicholson

Torridge Salmon
for H.F and T.H.

Soft light through cloud,
the dark ale river brimming its banks,
March hayfield overhead in the purpled alders.
And more jetsam of last week's spate,
an ash-tree complete, tossed out on the beach,
sprawling its forty feet, live swelling buds.
Young willow bark blushing into flame

by Island Run. There she might lie
under the streaming froth
she'd tasted down in Bideford Bay
and known no choice, only the urge
to leap and run against the flood,
seek out her natal gravel,
make it her bridal bed.

First searching casts self-conscious
until the head forgot to try,
let the body flow into the rod.
Then the line unrolled its loop,
the lure reached where the eyes looked,
swam slow past her window.
A petition was offered,
again and again.

Gentle, with soft-mouthing surprise,
with a gleam unexpectedly golden
deep in the stained pool,
she came for the feather
found the hook.
What followed was the craft of killing.
Her virgin scales cling to my hands.

Tom Rawling

The Trout Map

The Management Area of Cherokee
National Forest, interested in fish,
Has mapped Tellico and Bald Rivers
And North River, with the tributaries
Brookshire Branch and Sugar Cove Creek:
A fishy map for facile fishery

In Marvel's kind Ocean: drawn in two
Colors, blue and red—blue for the hue
Of Europe (Tennessee water is green),
Red lines by blue streams to warn
The fancy-fishmen from protected fish;
Black borders hold the Area in a cracked dish,

While other blacks, the dots and dashes, wire
The fisher's will through classic laurel
Over boar tracks to creamy pot-holes lying
Under Bald falls that thump the shying
Trout: we flew Professor, the Hackles and Worms.
(Tom Bagley and I were dotted and dashed wills.)

Up Green Cove gap from Preacher Millsap's cabin
We walked a confident hour of victory,
Sloped to the west on a trail that led us
To Bald River where map and scene were one
In seen-identity. Eight trout is the story
In three miles. We came to a rock-bridge

On which the road went left around a hill,
The river, right, tumbled into a cove;
But the map dashed the road along the stream
And we dotted man's fishiest enthymeme
With jellied feet upon understanding love
Of what eyes see not, that nourishes the will:

We were fishers, weren't we? And tried to fish
The egoed belly's dry cartograph—
Which made the government fish lie down and laugh.
(Tommy and I listened, we heard them shake
Mountain and cove because the map was fake.)
After eighteen miles our feet were clownish,

Then darkness took us into wheezing straits
Where coarse Magellan idling with his fates
Ran with the gulls for map around the Horn,
Or wheresoever the mind with tidy scorn
Revisits the world upon a dry sunbeam.
Now mapless the mountains were a dream.

                                        Allen Tate

The Twist in the River

At the clear, beer-coloured and bubbleshot twist in the river—
Every stone a speckled egg spawned in that deep lap,
Every pockmarked, pitted pebble a planet, blindly seeing through its
    own evolution—
The shallows, and the tall air, are filled with sound and light.
This part of the river expects to be seen, for it has drawn you there,
And the trees, selfless, introduced the sky into your love for the
    water.
If this place were a person, it would be making up a paper hat while
    humming,
Entirely self-contained, absorbed yet radiant—
A family moment, appearing normal until years later in retrospect,
When its depths are fully felt, beyond blunt experience.

Underwater, the light thickens slightly but never sets
And the river runs through its own fingers, careless.

Katherine Pierpoint

Two Rivulets

Two Rivulets side by side,
Two blended, parallel, strolling tides,
Companions, travelers, gossiping as they journey.

For the Eternal Ocean bound,
These ripples, passing surges, streams of Death and Life,
Object and Subject hurrying, whirling by,
The Real and Ideal,

Alternate ebb and flow the Days and Nights,
(Strands of a Trio twining, Present, Future, Past.)

In You, who'er you are, my book perusing;
In I myself—in all the World—these ripples flow,
All, all, toward the mystic Ocean tending.

(O yearnful waves! the kisses of your lips!
Your breast so broad, with open arms, O firm, expanded shore!)

Walt Whitman

A two-seater privy over a stream

All work, hitting at the buckled hills,
Stopped long ago. Trees have exploded
The dwelling house, but where they went and sat
Side by side for the resumption of innocence
Like pharaohs on two full moons
Their feet on a slate rest placidly
Their hands on their knees in the dry and out of the wind
(Except that the water shot through
Under their feet and moons and on the cold water
A colder draught was riding)
That place still stands. Well-built,
Homer would have called it, well-roofed.
The smooth wood is wormy but will support you.
I went in to eat an apple out of the rain.
Their bony hands. So high above Trawsfynydd
They had nobody upstream after the Romans left,
Always new water (after a rain
Like boiling quartz) and downstream not their worry.

David Constantine

Under the Waterfall

'Whenever I plunge my arm, like this,
In a basin of water, I never miss
The sweet sharp sense of a fugitive day
Fetched back from its thickening shroud of gray.
    Hence the only prime
    And real love-rhyme
    That I know by heart,
    And that leaves no smart,
Is the purl of a little valley fall
About three spans wide and two spans tall
Over a table of solid rock,
And into a scoop of the self-same block;
The purl of a runlet that never ceases
In stir of kingdoms, in wars, in peaces;
With a hollow boiling voice it speaks
And has spoken since hills were turfless peaks.'

'And why gives this the only prime
Idea to you of real love-rhyme?
And why does plunging your arm in a bowl
Full of spring water, bring throbs to your soul?'

'Well, under the fall, in a crease of the stone,
Though where precisely none ever has known,
Jammed darkly, nothing to show how prized,
And by now with its smoothness opalized,
    Is a drinking-glass:
    For, down that pass
    My lover and I
    Walked under a sky
Of blue with a leaf-wove awning of green,
In the burn of August, to paint the scene,
And we placed our basket of fruit and wine

By the runlet's rim, where we sat to dine;
And when we had drunk from the glass together,
Arched by the oak-copse from the weather,
I held the vessel to rinse in the fall,
Where it slipped, and sank, and was past recall,
Though we stooped and plumbed the little abyss
With long bared arms. There the glass still is.
And, as said, if I thrust my arm below
Cold water in a basin or bowl, a throe
From the past awakens a sense of that time,
And the glass we used, and the cascade's rhyme.
The basin seems the pool, and its edge
The hard smooth face of the brook-side ledge,
And the leafy pattern of china-ware
The hanging plants that were bathing there.

'By night, by day, when it shines or lours,
There lies intact that chalice of ours,
And its presence adds to the rhyme of love
Persistently sung by the fall above.
No lip has touched it since his and mine
In turns therefrom sipped lovers' wine.'

Thomas Hardy

Valley

after glass and slate sculpture by Meical Watts

In water-memory the river turns
always the same way at the boulder
and the bridge.
An ess of current at the land's shoulder,
the falling back of a sleeve where light burns
otter silk below the ridge.

A million million years of water-work
to make this place. A whispering seepage
through lion grass on fire
under snow. A stream's gleaming back
lifts from the mist and marshy weep
as flood meets deep and secret aquifers.

Dwyfor and Glaslyn, green-black rivers of the north
tumbling boulders for the walls of farms,
slip chisels of glass between the slate.
A rumour of ice, flood-fingers in sodden earth.
The bell of an old glacier in the rock's seams
so it splits clean at a tap of light.

Weather works the mountain to the bone
with the let juices of rain, the rising sea's erosion,
a river's gravity, flood's cold reflection,
a valley cut by water over stone.

Gillian Clarke

Vermilion Flycatcher, San Pedro River, Arizona

The river's been here, violent, right where we're standing,
you can tell by the trash caught overhead in the trees.
Now it's a trickle, and we're up to our knees
in late-spring yellowing weeds. A vermilion
flycatcher darts down, flutters up, perches.
Stick a pin in your thumb, the bead of blood
would be his colour. He's filled with joy
and the tranced rage of sex. How he conjures,
with his cry like a needle. A punctuation. A bone button

on fire. Everything bad you can imagine
is happening somewhere else, or happened
here, a hundred years or centuries
ago. He sings, and there's the murder:
you see it, forming under
the shimmering air, a man with brown
or white skin lying reversed
in the vanished water, a spear
or bullet in his back. At the ford, where the deer
come at dusk to cross and drink
and be ambushed. The red bird

is sitting on the same tree, intensely
bright in the sun that gleams on cruelty, on broken
skullbone, arrow, spur. Vultures cluster,
he doesn't care. He and his other-coloured mate
ignore everything but their own rapture.
Who knows what they remember?
Birds never dream, being their own.
Dreams, I mean. As for you, the river
that isn't there is the same one
you could drown in, face down.

Margaret Atwood

Vignette I

The sun comes up
like the outer husk
of some fiery despair.

The Ganga flows swollen with hymns.

Lepers huddle along the causeways
Like stunted shrubs
    black with frost-burns.
A thin dwarf, smeared blue with ash,
    spiked with a beard,
forested with matted hair,
cavorts ape-like. Overhead the monkeys gibber.
Crisp from their river-bath, women
drop coins in coconut-shells
but no avarice flickers
in the eyes of the palsied,
in the faces of the blind.

The river is a voice
in this desert of human lives.

A sail is hoisted,
the colour of musk-melon,
the colour of daggered flesh.
Beggars hoist their deformities
as boatmen hoist their sails.

The Ganga flows through the land,
not to lighten the misery
but to show it.

Keki N. Daruwalla

Vignette II

In the lower reaches of the sky
a lull of kites.

But along the river
you can feel the sound
      with your hands;
roll it along your mouth.
You can tell the time of the day
by it and the sharpness of frost
and whether the night was a river
          or a precipice.

Only the river doesn't speak here.
She is thought itself,
a soundless interior monologue.

Tonsured heads explode along
the water-surface.
All is spider-thread ritual here;
sandal-paste and *mantra*
chanting of the *gayatri*
shaved head and the *pinddan*.

You go the rounds of the *Panchtirath*
starting from the ghat where Durga
had dropped a sword
to where she dropped an earring
and the Panchganga Ghat where four rivers
are said to meet the Ganga,
like this river of faith going down
the stone-steps to meet the river.

Women do not take off their saris
as they enter the water;
men leave their clothes behind.
The dead leave their bodies.

Kites hang in the air
in suspended animation.
Shadows hang like birds on a dead wind.

A blind man's fingers grope across my face.
A sadhu eyes me unblinking from his navel.

Keki N. Daruwalla

mantra: incantatory verse
gayatri: sacred hymn intoned by Brahmins
pinddan: balls of rice symbolically offered to
   dead ancestors, but actually fed to cows
Panchtirath: the five sacred places in Varanasi

The Voice of the Rain

And who art thou? said I to the soft-falling shower,
Which, strange to tell, gave me an answer, as here translated:
I am the Poem of Earth, said the voice of the rain,
Eternal I rise impalpable out of the land and the bottomless sea,
Upward to heaven, whence, vaguely form'd, altogether changed,
   and yet the same,
I descend to lave the drouths, atomies, dust-layers of the globe,
And all that in them without me were seeds only, latent, unborn;
And forever, by day and night, I give back life to my own
   origin, and make pure and beautify it;
(For song, issuing from its birth-place, after fulfilment, wandering,
Reck'd or unreck'd, duly with love returns.)

Walt Whitman

The Watchers

By the ford at the town's edge
Horse and carter rest:
The carter smokes on the bridge
Watching the water press in swathes about his horse's chest.

From the inn one watches, too,
In the room for visitors
That has no fire, but a view
And many cases of stuffed fish, vermin, and kingfishers.

Edward Thomas

Water

I met an ancestor in the lane.
She couldn't stop: she was carrying water.
It slopped and bounced from the stoup against her;
the side of her skirt was dark with the stain,
oozing chillingly down to her shoe.
I stepped aside as she trudged past me,
frowning with effort, shivering slightly
(an icy drop splashed my foot too).
The dress that brushed against me was rough.
She didn't smell the way I smell:
I tasted the grease and smoke in her hair.
Water that's carried is never enough.
She'd a long haul back from the well.

No, I didn't see her. But she was there.

Fleur Adcock

The Water Below

This house is floored with water,
Wall to wall, a deep green pit,
Still and gleaming, edged with stone.
Over it are built stairways
And railed living-areas
In wrought iron. All rather
Impractical; it will be
Damp in winter, and we shall
Surely drop small objects—keys,
Teaspoons, or coins—through the chinks
In the ironwork, to splash
Lost into the glimmering
Depths (and do we know how deep?).
It will have to be rebuilt:
A solid floor of concrete
Over this dark well (perhaps
Already full of coins, like
The flooded crypt of that church
In Ravenna). You might say
It could be drained, made into
A useful cellar for coal.
But I am sure the water
Would return; would never go.
Under my grandmother's house
In Drury, when I was three,
I always believed there was
Water: lift up the floorboards
And you would see it—a lake,
A subterranean sea.
True, I played under the house
And saw only hard-packed earth,
Wooden piles, gardening tools,
A place to hunt for lizards.
That was different: below
I saw no water. Above,
I knew it must still be there,

Waiting. (For why did we say
'Forgive us our trespasses,
Deliver us from evil'?)
Always beneath the safe house
Lies the pool, the hidden sea
Created before we were.
It is not easy to drain
The waters under the earth.

Fleur Adcock

Water Colours

The trembling water glimpsed through dark tangle
Of late-month April's delicatest thorn,
One moment put the cuckoo-flower to scorn
Where its head hangs by sedges, Severn bank-full.
But dark water has a hundred fires on it;
As the sky changes it changes and ranges through
Sky colours and thorn colours, and more would do,
Were not the blossom truth so quick on it,
And beauty brief in action as first dew.

Ivor Gurney

The Water Diviner

Late, I have come to a parched land
doubting my gift, if gift I have,
the inspiration of water
spilt, swallowed in the sand.

To hear once more water trickle,
to stand in a stretch of silence

the divine pen twisting in the hand:
sign of depths alluvial.

Water owns no permanent shape,
brags, is most itself in chaos;
now, under the shadow of the idol,
dry mouth and dry landscape.

No rain falls with a refreshing sound
to settle tubular in a well,
elliptical in a bowl. No grape
lusciously moulds it round.

Clouds have no constant resemblance
to anything, blown by a hot wind,
flying mirages; the blue background,
light constructions of chance.

To hold back chaos I transformed
amorphous mass: clay, fire or cloud,
so that the agèd gods might dance
and golden structures form.

I should have built, plain brick on brick,
a water tower. The sun flies on
arid wastes, barren hells too warm,
and me with a hazel stick!

Rivulets vanished in the dust
long ago, great compositions
vaporised, salt on the tongue so thick
that drinking, still I thirst.

Repeated desert, recurring drought,
sometimes hearing water trickle,
sometimes not, I, by doubting first,
believe; believing, doubt.

Dannie Abse

The Water Diviner

You could say I embark on the land.
I move like a boat in the grip of water
That lives confidently, well below the wind.

Peaceful without sharks, with no tides turning,
Underneath tree roots and dead horses
It heaves through hell on a fine morning.

It is too deep to speak. It cannot be heard
Except by me, and I can hear it thinking
In a pun, a non sequitur, or a nonsense word.

I am a man erect in a town of impotents
A merchant banker among the feckless
A poet among civil servants.

This green field offers you a miracle.
You do not watch me, finding a stream
But all the water in the world shoving one mill.

Patricia Beer

Water Everywhere

Officially they do not acknowledge this god.
Officially they honour assorted immortals
In stone buildings with pioneering roofs.

Their houses betray them. Above ceilings,
Tanks for the precious stuff. Below, a shrine
To the godhead. Here they may stand alone

In confessional boxes, or lie full length
In his hollow bed, singing. Here he sometimes speaks
In loud, disquieting, oracular tones.

Fish are considered holy; where they go
We found contemplatives, with green umbrellas,
Making symbolic gestures at the stream.

In the hot month they consecrate their gardens
With a wet rite involving children, rubber, dogs.
On Sunday mornings they lustrate the car.

They pretend to disparage the god and his rainy gift,
Using set litanies: *Lovely weather for ducks!*
Last Thursday we had our summer. Flaming June!
(Black comedy is native to this people).

Daylong, nightlong, ministers of the god
Recite on different airways his moods and intentions.
The people claim not to believe. But they listen.

Their literature is great. They never read it.
Water, water everywhere the only
Line they can quote. Though ignorant of the context,
They reckon these words cover everything.

U. A. Fanthorpe

Water Meadows

Turn from this sleeping hill
whose blue and jagged edge
has cut the melting link
between earth and sky
to where a spectre fog
has blown abroad his breath,

rolled his steaming beard
across the patchwork plain.
A half-eyed world
within whose acred ease
centuries stand still,
each dew-splintered tree
has silence frail as death.

And now the sun-trapped mist
retreats upon the ridge
to crown again the peaks.
A far-off curlew calls
thin cries upon the wind.
A hidden stream
escaped from boom and tarn
rings clear its pebbled chimes
high over dreaming corn.
The huge theatre of earth
awakes to singing light.

Leonard Clark

Water Music

What I looked for was a place where water
Flowed continually. It could come
In rapids, over rocks in great falls and
Arrive at stillness far below. I watched
The hidden power. And then I went to rivers,
The source and mouth, the place where estuaries
Were the last, slow-moving waters and
The sea lay not far off continually
Making her music,
Loud gulls interrupting.

At first I only listened to her music,
Slow movements first, the held-back waves
With all their force to rear and roar and stretch
Over the waiting sand. Sea music is
What quiets my spirit. I would like my death
To come as rivers turn, as sea commands.
Let my last journey be to sounds of water.

Elizabeth Jennings

Watercourse

1.
Two inches deep and clear
    as nothing;
under it the small stones
    shine and are
magnified, mottled brown
    pointed with fire
where the sun strikes;
    follows declivities,
a flotation for grass-seeds
    insects specks of bark,
twisting into interstices
    of gravel, a tryout
for small sounds like
    the interlocking of vocables,
glistening flat and open
    holding some
of the sky's wide shine.

2.
The bubbled silence
    murmuring to itself enfolds
soft flutterings of air, sharp
    birdcries splintering off

the hill's solidity, a tractor's snore,
   the occasional seemingly
indigenous animal musings
   moaning across the pastures.

3.
The shine of a car strikes
   immovably. Already
a radio sheds into the air
   its flakes of music, its
chips of metalled voice.

4.
The river rattles past
   noisiest too in its
shallowest passages, almost
   able to stun
any alien sound.
   Later it scrabbles
at the motorway's even
   drum, climbing just
high enough to scarify
   that loud unmodified moan.

5.
When thickly it curdles
   through small towns
with froth blowing off it,
   opaque as toffee
and slow as November,
   the river loses.
Canalised and culverted
   directed underground
drained dammed utilised
   it enters silence.

6.
Water moves as language
    moves, building, eroding,
interfered with, trafficking
    helplessly with anything,
taking the colour of effluent,
    stifling the life of all
its organisms, flowing
    sterile, dropping inevitably
onward, necessary, dead.

7.
On the delta the marsh grass
    grows with its feet in a film
of light oil. This is the river's gift,
    its reluctant utterance;
colliding with the primal energies
    it limply spreads itself
to muffle the white ferocity of the tide-rip,
    to placate the salt.

John Cassidy

Watering Place

From pastureland I once dropped down
through a steep wood to where the sun
stopped in deep leaves before it lit
the floor, though a stream gathered it
and drew me, straying child, toward
music that light and water made . . .
I found the carcass of a ram
fallen across it, a queer dam;
dead weight, soft fleece of washing wool,
grub-addled matter in its shell.

With adult sense there on the brink
I dared to stoop, upstream, and drink.
But since, wading in sleep, I've fled
headlong, parched, sick, hoping to tread
water where nothing died, a source,
untarnished tarn where sheer falls slice
into iced water, mirrored heaven.
I'll not dip there awake. As then
I must cup hands close to the rot,
upstream, just, where the water's sweet.

Paul Hyland

Waterspout, 1853

They still ask me about the night
when the waterspout burst on Epynt.
I tell them little. It is enough
to have endured such workings of the mind,
to endure them still.

July heat grew heavier as afternoon
deepened; down over Builth the sky
was uneasy with cloud.
Midges thronged itchily by Duhonw stream.
The dog could not settle; prick-eared,
pelt a-twitch, whining,
he stared up at the hills.

Sultry night came. I woke to crazy howling,
clap after vicious clap of storm,
and growling, churning, pouring
greater far than rain.
I splashed across the kitchen,
fought whirlwind to get outside.
Lightning could not stop; it lit
luxuriance of destruction.

Across the demented stream—a torrent now,
tossing trees, rolling rocks, down, down
towards bloated Wye—I saw the house Dôlfach
split open, two contorted trees
passing through it and on.

All I saw, heard, darkly penetrated
all I was. Even now, long after,
I back away from questions. How
could I have helped them, the five who died?
I did not see them, and could not have heard.
Yet whatever years are left me
will be too few to build flood-walls
for my once inundated mind.

Ruth Bidgood

Well Water

What a girl called "the dailiness of life"
(Adding an errand to your errand. Saying,
"Since you're up . . ." Making you a means to
A means to a means to) is well water
Pumped from an old well at the bottom of the world.
The pump you pump the water from is rusty
And hard to move and absurd, a squirrel-wheel
A sick squirrel turns slowly, through the sunny
Inexorable hours. And yet sometimes
The wheel turns of its own weight, the rusty
Pump pumps over your sweating face the clear
Water, cold, so cold! you cup your hands
And gulp from them the dailiness of life.

Randall Jarrell

'Where is the sacred Well, that bore my Name?'

Where is the sacred Well, that bore my Name?
Fled to the Fountain back, from whence it came!
Fair Freedom's Emblem once, which smoothly flows,
And Blessings equally on all bestows.
Here, from the neighbouring Nursery of Arts,
The Students drinking, rais'd their Wit and Parts;
Here, for an Age and more, improv'd their Vein,
Their *Phoebus* I, my Spring their *Hippocrene*.
Discourag'd Youths, now all their Hopes must fail,
Condemn'd to Country Cottages and Ale;
To foreign Prelates make a slavish Court,
And by their Sweat procure a mean Support;
Or, for the Classicks read th'Attorney's Guide;
Collect Excise, or wait upon the Tide.

Jonathan Swift
from 'Verses occasioned by the sudden drying up
of St. Patrick's Well near Trinity College,
Dublin, in 1726 [1729?]'

'Where *Stour* receives her strength . . .'

Where *Stour* receives her strength from six cleere fountains fed,
Which gathering to one streame from every severall head,
Her new-beginning banke her water scarcely weelds:
And fairlie entreth first on the Dorsetian fields:
Where *Gillingham* with gifts that for a god were meet
(Enameled paths, rich wreaths, and every soveraine sweet
The earth and ayre can yeeld, and many a pleasure mixt)
Receives her. Whilst their past great kindness them betwixt,
The Forrest here bespoke; "How happie, Floods, are yee
From our predestin'd plagues that priviledged be,
Which onlie with the fish which in your banks doe breed,
And dailie there increase, man's gurmendize can feed?
But had this wretched age such uses to employ
Your waters, as the woods, we lately did enjoy,

194

Your chanels they would leave as barren by their spoil
As they of all our trees have latelie left our soil.
Insatiable Time thus all things doth devour:
Whatever saw the sunne that is not in Time's power?
Ye fleeting streames last long, out-living manie a day:
But, on more stedfast things Time makes the strongest prey."
Now towards the *Solent-sea*, as Stour her way doth ply,
On *Shaftesbury* (by chance) shee cast her crystal eye,
From whose foundation first, such strange reports arise
As brought into her mind the eagle's prophecies;
Of that so dreadfull plague, which all Great Britaine swept,
From that which highest flew to that which lowest crept,
Before the Saxon thence the Britaine should expell,
And all that thereupon successively befell.
How then the bloodie Dane subdued the Saxon race,
And, next, the Norman took possession of the place:
Those ages once expir'd, the fates to bring about,
The British line restored; the Norman linage out.
Then, those prodigious signs to ponder she began,
Which afterwards againe the Britans wrack fore-ran;
How here the owle at noon in public streets was seen,
As tho' the peopled towns had way-less deserts been.
And whilst the loathy toad out of his hole doth crawl,
And makes his fulsome stooll amid the prince's hall,
The crystall fountaine turn'd into a gory wound,
And bloodie issues brake (like ulcers) from the ground;
The seas against their course with double tides returne,
And oft were seene by night like boyling pitch to burne.
   Thus thinking, livelie Stour bestirres her tow'rds the maine;
Which *Lidden* leadeth out: then *Dulas* beares her traine
From Blackmore, that at once their watery tribute bring:
When, like some childish wench, she, looselie wantoning,
With tricks and giddie turnes seems to in-ile the shore
Betwixt her fishfull banks, that forward shee doth scour,
Until shee lastlie reach clear *Alen* in her race,
Which calmlie commeth down from her dear mother chace,
Of *Cranburn* that is call'd; who greatly joyes to see
A riveret borne of her for Stour's should reck'ned bee,
Of that renowned flood, a favourite highlie grac't.
   While Cranburn for her child so fortunatelie plac't,

With ecchoes everie way applauds her Alen's state,
A sudden noise from *Holt* seems to congratulate
With Cranburn for her brooke so happily bestow'd:
Where to her neighboring chase, the curteous forrest show'd
So just conceived joy, that from each rising hurst,
Where many a goodlie oake had carefullie been nurst,
The sylvans in their songs their mirthfull meetings tell,
And satires, that in slades and gloomy dimbles dwell,
Runne whooting to the hills to clappe their ruder hands.
  As Holt had done before, so *Canford*'s goodlie launds
(Which leene upon the Poole) enricht with coppras vaines,
Rejoice to see them join'd. When downe from Sarum plaines
Cleare *Avon* comming in her sister Stour doth call,
And at New Forrest's foote into the sea doe fall.

Michael Drayton
from 'Second Song'—Polyolbion

'Who carved a bird and a fish'

*Commissioned for the opening of The Museum
of Scotland, 30 November 1998*

Who carved a bird and a fish
on a standing stone?
What kind of a fish?
An Alec, a Bream, a Burt, a Char,
a Cunner, a Cusk, a Dab, a Dace, a Drumfish
that swam in the Dee, the Don, the Spey,
the Tay, the Forth, the Annan, the Nith,
the Clyde and the Tweed
before these rivers were words—
before the bird was a word,
though your finger tracing its shape
in the stone
knows it's a géadh, a goose.

Carol Ann Duffy
from Standing Stone, Part 1

'Wide o'er the Brim, with many a Torrent swell'd'

Wide o'er the Brim, with many a Torrent swell'd,
And the mix'd Ruin of its Banks o'erspread,
At last the rous'd-up River pours along:
Resistless, roaring, dreadful, down it comes,
From the rude Mountain, and the mossy Wild,
Tumbling thro' Rocks abrupt, and sounding far;
Then o'er the sanded Valley floating spreads,
Calm, sluggish, silent; till again constrain'd
Between two meeting Hills it bursts a Way,
Where Rocks and Woods o'erhang the turbid Stream;
There gathering triple Force, rapid, and deep,
It boils, and wheels, and foams, and thunders' thro'.

James Thompson
from The Seasons

The Wounded Otter

A wounded otter
on a bare rock,
a bolt in her side,
stroking her whiskers,
stroking her webbed feet.

Her ancestors
told her once
that there was a river,
a crystal river,
a waterless bed.

They also said
there were trout there
fat as tree-trunks
and kingfishers
bright as blue spears—

men there without cinders
in their boots,
men without dogs
on leashes.

She did not notice
the world die
nor the sun expire.
She was already
swimming at ease
in the magic crystal river.

Michael Hartnett

The Wye Below Bredwardine

The banks are steep. Drought. Water too low.
Too many trees by it too, it feels. Yet
They impress heavily, this hot calm day.
Trees hang and bulge over, and peer right down.
Thirsty alders lean over, the bane of water.

Huge plate-glass windows sliding along
Horizontally, slowly rotate as they go. No
Hurry in such drift. And when flies and seeds
Hit it, dartboards widen and meet the dead
Hauteur of the banks, their raw nettle clumps.

Lower down these panes bump submerged reefs,
Lazily give, yet resist quite breaking.
Little folds and pleats adjust the Wye's surface.
Leaning over you see its tiny corkscrewings,
Like pocks on estuary mud, but down water.

Suddenly, near one bank in a patch of weedy
Sunlight, a blue shoal of chub. And,
Several feet down by the bridge's piles, one
Salmon flickered deep like a neon light.
Swinging on a branch, a tyre half-submerged.

What ease has this tonnage of sedately moving
Water. Sleepily it stirs, then enfolded
With so slight a turn rolls over in bed and
Weighs sideways down again. A hundred metres
Wide. Leaves, bubbles, downy stuff, flies.

It is evening sunlight. Already. Lambs baa.
I love you sylvan Wye, or would do so,
If that were tenable, correct, and still allowed.
Instead, I say too many trees. Traherne himself
Imagined this heaven. Is there hope? Swans arrive.

John Powell Ward

Acknowledgements

Our especial thanks go to all of the poets simply for writing what they write and for stimulating new thoughts, widening our horizons and giving us courage.

We thank all the poets, publishers and literary executors who have generously allowed us to include poems without fee and have introduced us to other poems and poets in their enthusiasm. Many have suggested poems—thank you to Darren Giddings, Jane Kendall, Rupert Nabarro, Steve Turner, Karen Wimhurst, Bloodaxe in Newcastle, Chelsea Green in White River Junction, Vermont, The Gallery Press in County Meath, and Copper Canyon Press in Washington State.

There are many poems which we could not include: some because they were simply too long, some because despite months of writing for permissions no one wrote back to us, and some because of the sums asked for by publishers and agents. The permissions jungle is so fraught now, because of understaffed copyright departments and demanding corporate mentalities, it takes away much of the pleasure and a good deal of the point. But then one phone call from a friendly poet or publisher raises the spirits once more.

It has been serendipitous that our fellow founder-director of Common Ground, Roger Deakin, has also been immersed in rivers. We are very grateful to him and fortunate that he has been able to find time to write the Foreword at a time when his book *Waterlog: A Swimmer's Journey through Britain* has been published to critical acclaim. His book celebrates the good people and places along our rivers and coasts, and quietly insists that we join those trying to improve the rest— an aspiration we share. We are lucky in having a Board of very supportive Trustees; our thanks to all of them.

Clifford Harper has once more created a great cover illustration, and we have to thank James Crowden for the words that became our title: 'The River's Voice', which recurs in his book about the River Parrett, *In Time of Flood*.

Angela did most of the typesetting with help from Jane Kendall; thanks to her also for proofreading again and again and then again.

We must thank John Elford at Green Books, who deserved better. His patience and good humour were sorely tried, as we called yet again to say that permissions still had not arrived.

The Poetry Library, full of twentieth-century works, has again been an invaluable source despite competition with fellow shelf rollers. Situated on the fifth floor of the Festival Hall on the south bank of the Thames, it is an inspiring place to walk to if you concentrate on the great river. The library at Swiss Cottage filled many gaps with the older poems, but Camden Council is not alone in trying to close libraries. Why is it such a struggle to be widely read?

Although we have achieved this book in our own time, we should like to thank the Baring Foundation, English Nature, Esmée Fairbairn Charitable Trust and others for their support of our formative work on Rhynes, Rivers and Running Brooks, out of which has flowed not only this book, but our pioneering model project Confluence, funded mainly by the Arts Lottery's programme 'Arts for Everyone', in which we are helping local people make music for a river: the Stour in Somerset, Wiltshire and Dorset.

We do hope that if there are any mistakes, you will tell us and forgive us; doing things in between and on a shoestring should be no excuse. The following pages form an extension of the copyright page. We have tried very hard to trace copyright holders—we apologize if there are any omissions or mistakes, and would be grateful if you could write to us so that we can correctly attribute and thank the people concerned.

Angela King and Susan Clifford
Common Ground

A–Z List of Poets and their Poems with Sources and Acknowledgements

Abse, Dannie, 1923–
  The Water Diviner
  Selected Poems, Hutchinson, 1970. © Dannie Abse 1970.
  Reproduced by permission of the author.

Adcock, Fleur, 1934–
  River
  The Water Below
  Selected Poems, Oxford University Press, 1983.

  Water
  Looking Back, Oxford University Press, 1997. © Fleur Adcock,
  1983/1997. Reproduced by permission of Oxford University Press.

Ammons, A. R., 1926–
  If Anything Will Level with You Water Will
  The Selected Poems, Expanded Edition. © 1987, 1977,
  1975, 1974, 1972, 1971, 1970, 1966, 1965, 1964, 1955 by
  A.R. Ammons. Reprinted by permission of W. W. Norton &
  Company, Inc.

  Flat Rock
  Brink Road, copyright © 1996 by A. R. Ammons. Reprinted by
  permission of W. W. Norton & Company, Inc.

Atwood, Margaret, 1939–
  River
  The Animals in that Country. Toronto: Oxford University Press
  Canada, 1968. Reprinted by permission of Oxford University
  Press Canada and Curtis Brown Ltd.

  Vermillion Flycatcher, San Pedro River, Arizona
  Eating Fire, Selected Poetry, 1965–1995, Virago, 1998.
  © Margaret Atwood 1968/1998. Reproduced by permission of
  Curtis Brown.

Auden, W. H., 1907–1973
  River Profile
  Collected Poems by W. H. Auden, edited by Edward Mendelson.
  Copyright © 1966 by W. H. Auden. Reprinted by permission of
  Random House, Inc. *Collected Poems*, Faber, 1976. Reproduced
  by permission of Faber & Faber and Curtis Brown Ltd.

Beer, Patricia, 1924–1999
   The Estuary
   The Water Diviner
   Collected Poems, Carcanet Press, 1998. © Patricia Beer 1998.
   Reproduced by permission of Carcanet Press.

Bellerby, Frances, 1899–1975
   First Day of September
   Selected Poems, Enitharmon, 1986. Reprinted by permission of
   Charles Causley.

Berry, Wendell, 1934–
   The Porch over the River
   Collected Poems 1957–82, North Point Press, 1984. © Wendell
   Berry 1984. Reproduced by permission of the author.

   The Springs
   Selected Poems, Counterpoint Press, 1998. © Wendell Berry
   1998. Reprinted by permission of Perseus Books Group/
   Counterpoint Press and the author.

Betjeman, John, 1906–1984
   'Gentle Brent I used to know you'
   from 'Middlesex', *Collected Poems*, John Murray, 1958/70.
   Reproduced by permission of John Murray (Publishers) Ltd.

Bidgood, Ruth, 1922–
   Waterspout, 1853
   The Fluent Moment, Seren Books, 1996. © Ruth Bidgood 1996.
   Reproduced by permission of the author.

Bishop, Elizabeth, 1911–1979
   'There are too many waterfalls here. . .'
   from 'Questions of Travel', *The Complete Poems 1927–1979*.
   Copyright © 1979, 1983 by Alice Helen Methfessel. Reprinted
   by permission of Farrar, Straus and Giroux, LLC, and Chatto &
   Windus.

Blake, William 1757–1827
   XII Song
   from 'Poetical Sketches', *The Poems of William Blake*, edited by
   W. H. Stevenson, Longman 1971.

Brackenbury, Alison, 1953–
   The Spring at Chedworth
   1829, Carcanet Press, 1995. © Alison Brackenbury 1995.
   Reproduced by permission of the author and Carcanet Press.

Burns, Robert, 1759–1796
    The Banks of Nith
    The Poetical Works of Robert Burns, edited by John Fawside,
    Bliss, Sands & Foster, 1896.

Burnside, John, 1955–
    In Avon
    The Myth of the Twin, Cape Poetry, 1994. © John Burnside
    1994. Reproduced by permission of the author and Random
    House UK Ltd.

Byard, Olivia, 1946–
    Scotland in an Oxford Landscape
    A Benediction, Peterloo Poets, 1997. © Olivia Byard 1997.
    Reproduced by permission of Peterloo Poets.

Carew, Thomas, ?1595–1639
    To my Mistris sitting by a Rivers side. An Eddy.
    The Poems of Thomas Carew, edited by Rhodes Dunlop,
    Oxford University Press, 1949.

Carruth, Hayden, 1921–
    The Brook
    Scrambled Eggs & Whiskey, Copper Canyon Press, 1996.
    © Hayden Carruth, 1996. Reproduced by permission of Copper
    Canyon Press.

Cassidy, John, 1928–
    Watercourse
    Night Cries, Bloodaxe Books, 1982. © John Cassidy 1982.
    Reproduced by permission of Bloodaxe Books.

Causley, Charles, 1917–
    Sibard's Well
    Collected Poems 1951–1997, Macmillan, 1997.
    © Charles Causley 1997. Reproduced by permission of the
    author and David Higham Associates.

Clare, John, 1793–1864
    The Ford
    Round Oak and Eastwell
    Rustic Fishing
    The Poems of John Clare, edited by J. W. Tibble, Dent, 1935.
    Reproduced by permission of The Orion Publishing Group Ltd.

Clark, Leonard, 1905–1981
    Forest Pools
    Selected Poems 1940–1957, Hutchinson, 1958.

    Water Meadows
    The Way it Was—Poems by Leonard Clark, Enitharmon, 1980.
    Reproduced by permission of the Literary Estate of Leonard
    Clark.

Clarke, Gillian, 1937–
    St Winefride's Well
    Collected Poems, Carcanet Press, 1997.

    Valley
    Five Fields, Carcanet Press, 1998. © Gillian Clarke 1997/1998.
    Reproduced by permission of Carcanet Press.

Coleridge, Samuel Taylor, 1772–1834
    Inscription for a Fountain on a Heath
    Sonnet to the River Otter
    The Poems of Samuel Taylor Coleridge, Bradbury & Evans, 1852.

Conn, Stewart, 1936–
    Lothian Burn
    from 'Pentland Poems', *Stolen Light, Selected Poems*, Bloodaxe
    Books, 1999. © Stewart Conn 1999. Reproduced by permission
    of Bloodaxe Books.

Constantine, David, 1944–
    A two-seater privy over a stream
    Selected Poems, Bloodaxe Books, 1991. © David Constantine
    1991. Reproduced by permission of Bloodaxe Books.

Cornford, Frances, 1886–1960
    In the Backs
    Selected Poems, Enitharmon Press, 1996.
    Reproduced by permission of Enitharmon Press.

Crane, Hart, 1899–1932
    Repose of Rivers
    Complete Poems of Hart Crane edited by Marc Simon.
    Copyright © 1933, 1958, 1966 by Liveright Publishing
    Corporation. Copyright © 1986 by Marc Simon. Reprinted by
    permission of Liveright Publishing Corporation. Bloodaxe
    Books, 1984.

Crowden, James 1954–
Downstream Effects: River Stour
Springhead at Fontmell Magna
© James Crowden 1999. Reproduced by permission of the author.

Crucefix, Martyn, 1956–
The Fisherman
A Madder Ghost, Enitharmon Press, 1997. © Martyn Crucefix 1997. Reproduced by permission of the author and Enitharmon Press.

Cullup, Michael
Heaven
Reading Geographies, Carcanet Press, 1982. © Michael Cullup 1982. Reproduced by permission of Carcanet Press.

Dale, Peter, 1938–
Not Drinking Water
Edge to Edge—New and Selected Poems, Anvil Press Poetry, 1996. © Peter Dale, 1996. Reproduced by permission of Anvil Press Poetry.

Daruwalla, Keki N., 1937–
Vignette I
Vignette II
Crossing of Rivers and the Keeper of the Dead, Oxford University Press, 1991. © Keki Daruwalla 1991. Reprinted by permission of Oxford University Press, New Delhi.

Davie, Donald, 1922–1995
Green River
Selected Poems, Carcanet Press, 1992.
Reproduced by permission of Carcanet Press.

Denham, Sir John, 1615–1699
The Thames
Penguin Book of English Verse, edited by John Hayward, 1956.

Dickinson, Emily, 1830–1886
'Like Rain it sounded till it curved'
Reprinted by permission of the publishers and the Trustees of Amherst College from *The Poems of Emily Dickinson*, Ralph W. Franklin, ed., Cambridge, Mass.; The Belknap Press of Harvard University Press, copyright © 1998 by the President and Fellows of Harvard College, copyright © 1951, 1955, 1979 by the President and Fellows of Harvard College.

Donne, John, 1572–1613
The Baite
Donne—Poetry & Prose, Oxford University Press, 1946/1960.

Dooley, Maura, 1957–
Net and River
Kissing a Bone, Bloodaxe Books, 1996. © Maura Dooley 1996.
Reproduced by permission of Bloodaxe Books.

Downar, Joan, 1930–?
River People
The Empire of Light, Harry Chambers/Peterloo Poets, 1984.
Reproduced by permission of Peterloo Poets.

Drayton, Michael, 1563–1631
'Where *Stour* receives her strength . . .'
from *Polyolbion—Second Song*.

Duffy, Carol Ann, 1955–
River
The Other Country, Anvil Press Poetry, 1990.

'Who carved a bird and a fish'
from 'Standing Stone', *The Pamphlet*, Anvil Press Poetry, 1998.
© Carol Ann Duffy 1990/1998. Reproduced by permission of
Anvil Press Poetry.

Dunbar, William, 1465–1530?
'Above all rivers thy river hath renown'
from 'To the City of London', *Poems on the Underground*, new
and extended edition, edited by Gerard Benson, Judith Chernaik
and Cicely Herbert, Cassell Publishers Ltd, 1994. Reproduced
by permission of The Orion Publishing Group Ltd.

Dunmore, Helen, 1952–
Hungry Thames
Bestiary, Bloodaxe Books, 1997. © Helen Dunmore 1997.
Reproduced by permission of Bloodaxe Books.

Dunn, Douglas, 1942–
Tay Bridge
Northlight, Faber & Faber, 1988. © Douglas Dunn 1988.
Reproduced by permission of Faber & Faber and Peters, Fraser
and Dunlop.

Dutton, G. F., 1924–
   Bridge
   The Concrete Garden, Bloodaxe Books, 1991.
   © G.F. Dutton 1991. Reproduced by permission of Bloodaxe
   Books.

Eliot, T. S., 1888–1965
   'The river's tent is broken: the last fingers of leaf'
   from 'The Fire Sermon', *The Waste Land, Collected Poems
   1909–1935*, Faber & Faber, 1936.

Fallon, Peter, 1951–
   The River
   News of the World, Selected and New Poems, Gallery Books,
   1998. © Peter Fallon 1998. Reproduced by permission of the
   author.

Fanthorpe, U. A., 1929–
   Rising Damp
   Standing To, Peterloo Poets, 1985.

   Water Everywhere
   Safe as Houses, Peterloo Poets, 1995.
   © U. A. Fanthorpe 1985/1995. Reproduced by permission of
   Peterloo Poets.

Fisher, Roy, 1930–
   Abstracted Water
   Birmingham River
   Birmingham River, Oxford University Press, 1994.
   © Roy Fisher 1994. Reproduced by permission of the author.

Frost, Robert, 1874–1963
   A Brook in the City
   The Complete Poems of Robert Frost, Cape, 1951. Reproduced
   by permission of Random House UK Ltd. From *The Poetry of
   Robert Frost*, edited by Edward Connery Lathem, copyright ©
   1951 by Robert Frost. Copyright © 1923, 1969 by Henry Holt
   and Company, LLC. Reprinted by permission of Henry Holt &
   Co, LLC.

Fuller, John, 1937–
   Boundaries
   Collected Poems, Chatto & Windus, 1997.
   © John Fuller 1997. Reprinted by permission of the author.

Galvin, James, 1951–
    At the Sand Creek Bridge
    'How shy the attraction'
    from 'Water Table', *Resurrection Update*, Copper Canyon Press.
    © James Galvin 1997. Reproduced by permission of the Copper
    Canyon Press.

Garfitt, Roger, 1944–
    Culvert
    Given Ground, Carcanet Press, 1989. © Roger Garfitt 1989.
    Reproduced by permission of Carcanet Press.

Greening, John, 1954–
    Beside the Wye
    Huntingdonshire Eclogues I
    An Offering
    Fotheringhay and other Poems, Rockingham Press, 1995.
    © John Greening 1995. Reproduced by permission of the
    author.

Greenlaw, Lavinia, 1962–
    River History
    Night Photographs, Faber & Faber, 1993. © Lavinia Greenlaw
    1993. Reproduced by permission of Faber & Faber.

Gurney, Ivor, 1890–1937
    The Soaking
    Water Colours
    The Collected Poems of Ivor Gurney, edited by P. J. Kavanagh,
    Oxford University Press, 1984. Reproduced by permission of
    the Oxford University Press.

Hamburger, Michael, 1924–
    Thames
    Collected Poems 1941–1994, Anvil Press Poetry, 1995.
    © Michael Hamburger 1995. Reproduced by permission of
    Anvil Press Poetry and the author.

Hardy, Thomas, 1840–1928
    On Sturminster Foot-Bridge
    Under the Waterfall
    The Complete Poems, edited by James Gibson, Macmillan,
    1976/1979.

Hartnett, Michael, 1941–
    The Poet as Spirit of the River
    Collected Poems, The Gallery Press (forthcoming).

    The Wounded Otter
    Selected & New Poems, The Gallery Press, 1994.
    © Michael Hartnett 1994. Reproduced by permission of The
    Gallery Press.

Heaney, Seamus, 1939–
    Anahorish
    Opened Ground—Selected Poems 1966–96, Faber & Faber,
    1998. Copyright © by Seamus Heaney 1998. Reprinted by
    permission of Farrar, Straus and Giroux, LLC, and Faber & Faber.

    'The Riverbed . . .'
    The Haw Lantern, Faber & Faber, 1982. © Seamus Heaney
    1982/1990. Reproduced by permission of Faber & Faber.

Heath-Stubbs, John, 1918–
    River Song
    Collected Poems 1943–1982, Carcanet Press, 1988.
    © John Heath-Stubbs 1988. Reproduced by permission of David
    Higham Associates.

Henri, Adrian, 1932–
    Angler
    Collected Poems, Allison & Busby, 1986. © Adrian Henri 1986.
    Reproduced by permission of Allison and Busby Ltd.

Herrick, Robert, 1591–1674
    Dean-bourn, *a rude River* in Devon, *by which sometimes he lived*
    The Poetical Works of Robert Herrick, edited by F. W. Moorman,
    Clarendon Press, Oxford, 1915.

Hesketh, Phoebe, 1909–
    Kingfisher
    The River Idle
    Netting the Sun, New and Collected Poems, Enitharmon Press,
    1989. © Phoebe Hesketh 1989. Reproduced by permission of
    Enitharmon Press.

Hooker, Jeremy, 1941–
    Guests of Silence
    Our Lady of Europe, Enitharmon Press, 1997. © Jeremy
    Hooker 1997. Reproduced by permission of Enitharmon Press.

Hopkins, Gerard Manley, 1844–1889
Penmaen Pool
Poems and Prose of Gerard Manley Hopkins, selected and
edited by W. H. Gardner, Penguin Books, 1953.

Housman, A. E., 1859–1936
'Clunton and Clunbury'
from 'A Shropshire Lad', *The Collected Poems of A. E. Housman*,
Jonathan Cape, 1939/79. Reproduced by permission of the
Society of Authors as the literary representative of the Estate of
A. E. Housman.

Hughes, Ted, 1930–1999
An Eel
New Selected Poems 1957–1994, Faber & Faber, 1995.
Reproduced by permission of Faber & Faber.

Hyland, Paul, 1947–
Drouth End
Watering Place
The Stubborn Forest, Bloodaxe Books, 1984. © Paul Hyland
1984. Reproduced by permission of the author and David
Higham Associates.

Jarrell, Randall, 1914–1965
Well Water
The Complete Poems, Faber & Faber, 1971. Reprinted by
permission of Faber & Faber. *The Complete Poems* by Randall
Jarrell. Copyright © 1969 and copyright renewed © 1997 by
Mary von S. Jarrell. Reprinted by permission of Farrar, Straus
and Giroux, LLC.

Joseph, Jenny, 1932–
River rising in India
Selected Poems, Bloodaxe Books, 1992. © Jenny Joseph 1992.
Reproduced by permission of the author.

Jennings, Elizabeth, 1926–
Water Music
Collected Poems 1953–1985, Carcanet Press, 1986.
© Elizabeth Jennings 1986. Reproduced by permission of David
Higham Associates.

Lawrence, D. H., 1885–1930
    Embankment at Night Before the War—Outcasts
    The Third Thing
    The Complete Poems of D. H. Lawrence, edited by V. de Sola
    Pinto and F. W. Roberts, Penguin Books, 1964. Reproduced by
    permission of Laurence Pollinger Limited and the Estate of
    Frieda Lawrence Ravagli. © 1964, 1971 by Angelo Ravagli and
    C. M. Weekley, Executors of the Estate of Frieda Lawrence
    Ravagli. Used by permission of Viking Penguin, a division of
    Penguin Putnam Inc.

Levertov, Denise, 1923–1998
    Sands of the Well
    Sands of the Well, Bloodaxe Books, 1994/1998. Copyright ©
    Denise Levertov 1996. Reprinted by permission of New
    Directions Publishing Corp.

Levi, Peter, 1931–
    Rivers
    Collected Poems 1955–1975, Anvil Press Poetry, 1984. © Peter
    Levi 1984. Reproduced by permission of Anvil Press Poetry.

Llewellyn-Williams, Hilary, 1951–
    Behind the Waterfall
    Mother Anthony's
    Animaculture, Seren Books, 1997. © Hilary Llewellyn-Williams
    1997. Reproduced by permission of the author.

Longfellow, H. W., 1807–1882
    To the River Charles
    The Poetical Works of H.W. Longfellow, Collins Clear-Type
    Press, n.d.

Longley, Michael, 1939–
    Spring Tide
    Poems 1963–1983, The Salamander Press/Gallery Press, 1985.
    © Michael Longley 1985. Reprinted by permission of the author.

Lowell, Robert, 1917–1977
    The Charles River (1)
    Notebook, Faber & Faber, 1974. Reproduced by permission of
    Faber & Faber. *For Lizzie and Harriet* by Robert Lowell.
    Copyright © 1973 by Robert Lowell. Reprinted by permission
    of Farrar, Straus and Giroux, LLC.

MacCaig, Norman, 1910–1996
Dipper
Gray Wagtail
Kingfisher
Collected Poems, Chatto & Windus, 1993. Reproduced by
permission of Random House UK Ltd.

MacColl, Ewan
Sweet Thames Flow Softly
© 1996 Sweet Thames Flow Softly by Ewan MacColl, Harmony
Music Ltd, 11 Uxbridge Street, London w8 7TQ.

MacDiarmid, Hugh, 1892–1978
The Salmon Leap
Complete Poems, edited by Michael Grieve and W. R. Aitken,
Carcanet Press, 1993. Reproduced by permission of Carcanet
Press.

Mahon, Derek, 1941–
The Banished Gods
Heraclitus on Rivers
Collected Poems, Gallery Books, 1999. © Derek Mahon 1999.
Reproduced by permission of the author and The Gallery Press.

Mandelstam, Osip, 1891–1938
'The factories, bathing in the Moscow river'
The Moscow Notebooks, translated by Richard and Elizabeth
McKane, Bloodaxe Books, 1991. Reproduced by permission of
Bloodaxe Books.

Marvell, Andrew, 1621–1678
The Kingfisher
The Penguin Book of English Verse, edited by John Hayward,
1956.

The River Meadows (In Flood)
The Life and Lyrics of Andrew Marvell by Michael Craze,
Macmillan 1979.

Mills, Paul, 1948–
The Launch
Half Moon Bay, Carcanet Press, 1993. © Paul Mills 1993.
Reproduced by permission of Carcanet Press.

Milton, John, 1608–1674
'Rivers arise; whether thou be the Son'
Milton—Poems, Dent, 1959. Reproduced by permission of The
Orion Publishing Group Ltd.

Minhinnick, Robert, 1952–
 Eels at Night
 Sap
 A Thread in the Maze, Christopher Davies, Swansea, 1978.
 © Robert Minhinnick 1978. Reproduced by permission of
 Carcanet Press.

Montague, John, 1929–
 Springs
 Collected Poems, The Gallery Press, 1995. © John Montague
 1995. Reproduced by permission of The Gallery Press.

Morgan, Edwin, 1920–
 The Dowser
 Themes on a Variation, Carcanet Press, 1988. © Edwin Morgan
 1998. Reproduced by permission of Carcanet Press.

Morrison, Blake, 1950–
 Flood
 Dark Glasses, Chatto & Windus, 1989. © Blake Morrisson
 1989. Reprinted by permission of Peters Fraser and Dunlop
 Group Ltd.

Motion, Andrew, 1952–
 'Now the children are old enough . . .'
 from 'Fresh Water', *Salt Water*, Faber & Faber, 1997.
 © Andrew Motion 1997. Reproduced by permission of Faber &
 Faber.

Murdoch, Iris 1919–1999
 October
 A Year of Birds, Chatto & Windus, 1984. Reprinted by
 permission of the Estate of Iris Murdoch and Ed Victor Ltd.

Murphy, Richard, 1927–
 Brian Boru's Well
 New Selected Poems, Faber & Faber, 1989. © Richard Murphy
 1989. Reproduced by permission of the author.

Nicholson, Norman, 1914–1987
 Beck
 Five Rivers
 Collected Poems, Faber & Faber, 1994.

 To the River Duddon
 Selected Poems 1940–1982, Faber & Faber, 1982.
 Reproduced by permission of David Higham Associates.

Ormond, John, 1923–1990
Definition of a Waterfall
Salmon
Selected Poems, Seren Books, 1987. Reproduced by permission of Glenys Ormond Thomas.

Oswald, Alice, 1966–
Otter Out and In
The Thing in the Gap-Stone Stile, Oxford University Press, 1996. © Alice Oswald 1996. Reproduced by permission of the author and Oxford University Press.

River
First published by Secret Gardens, 1999, in association with the Salisbury Festival. © Alice Oswald 1999. Reproduced by permission of the The Poetry Society and the author.

Owen, Wilfred, 1893–1917
Shadwell Stair
The Collected Poems of Wilfred Owen, edited by C. Day Lewis, Chatto & Windus, 1964. Reproduced by permission of Random House UK Ltd.

Oxley, William, 1939–
Liffey Water
The Green Crayon Man, Rockingham Press, 1997.
© William Oxley 1997. Reproduced by permission of The Rockingham Press.

Pierpoint, Katherine, 1961–
The Twist in the River
Truffle Beds, Faber & Faber, 1995. © Katherine Pierpoint 1995. Reproduced by permission of Faber & Faber.

Pope, Alexander, 1688–1744
The River
Poetical Works, edited by Herbert Davis, Oxford University Press, 1996.

Porteous, Katrina, 1960–
Long Nanny Burn
Team Gut
The Lost Music, Bloodaxe Books, 1996. © Katrina Porteous 1996. Reproduced by permission of the author and Bloodaxe Books.

Powell, Neil, 1948–
    Hundred River
    Selected Poems, Carcanet Press, 1998. © Neil Powell 1998.
    Reproduced by permission of Carcanet Press.

Prynne, J. H., 1936–
    Along Almost Any River
    Force of Circumstance and other Poems, Routledge & Kegan
    Paul Ltd, 1962. © J. H. Prynne 1962. Reproduced by
    permission of Routledge.

Raine, Craig, 1944–
    Floods
    A Martian Sends a Postcard Home, Oxford University Press,
    1979. © Craig Raine 1979. Reproduced by permission of the
    author.

Rawling, Tom, 1916–1996
    The Names of the Sea-Trout
    Torridge Salmon
    The Names of the Sea-Trout, Littlewood Arc, 1993.
    Reproduced by permission of Mrs. Sue Slater and Rev. Jane
    Rawling.

Rich, Adrienne, 1929–
    Concord River
    Selected Poems by Adrienne Rich, Chatto & Windus, 1967.
    Collected Early Poems: 1950–1970, W. W. Norton & Company,
    Inc. Copyright © 1993, 1955 by Adrienne Rich. Reprinted by
    permission of the author and W. W. Norton & Company, Inc.

Scannell, Vernon, 1922–
    A Day on the River
    Collected Poems 1950–1993, Robson Books, 1993. © Vernon
    Scannell 1993. Reproduced by permission of the author.

Sail, Lawrence, 1942–
    Riverine
    Devotions, Secker & Warburg, 1987. © Lawrence Sail 1987.
    Reprinted by permission of Random House UK Ltd.

Shakespeare, William, 1564–1616
    'There is a willow grows aslant a brook'
    Hamlet, Act 4 Scene 7.

Shelley, Percy Bysshe, 1792–1822
    The Question

Smith, Stevie, 1902–1971
The River God
Collected Poems of Stevie Smith, Penguin 20th Century Classics, 1975. Copyright © 1972 by Stevie Smith. Reprinted by permission of New Directions Publishing Corp. and James MacGibbon.

Snyder, Gary, 1930–
Fording the Flooded Goldie River
Left out in the Rain, New Poems 1947–1985, North Point Press, 1986. Copyright © 1986 by Gary Snyder. Reprinted by permission of the author and North Point Press, a division of Farrar, Straus and Giroux LLC.

River in the Valley
Axe Handles. Copyright © 1983 by Gary Snyder. Reprinted by permission of the author and North Point Press, a division of Farrar, Straus and Giroux, LLC.

Spenser, Edmund, 1552–1599
'So went he playing on the watery plaine'
The Faerie Queene, edited by P. Roche Jr and Patrick O'Donnell Jr, Penguin, 1978.

Steer, Bernie
Dockland
London Lines, 'Places and Faces of London in Poetry and Song', selected by Kenneth Baker, Methuen, 1982. © Bernie Steer 1982.

Stevens, Wallace, 1879–1955
The River of Rivers in Connecticut
The Collected Poems of Wallace Stevens, copyright © 1954 by Wallace Stevens. Reprinted by permission of Alfred A. Knopf, Inc., a Division of Random House Inc. and Faber & Faber.

Stevenson, Anne, 1933–
A River
The Collected Poems of Anne Stevenson, 1955–1995, Oxford University Press, 1996. © Anne Stevenson 1996. Reproduced by permission of the author.

Swift, Jonathan 1667–1745
'Where is the sacred Well, that bore my Name?'
from 'Verses occasioned by the sudden drying up of St. Patrick's Well near Trinity College, Dublin in 1726 [1729?]'. *Swift—Poetical Works*, Oxford University Press 1967.

Tate, Allen, 1899–1979
   The Trout Map
   Collected Poems 1919–1976. Copyright © 1977 by Allen Tate.
   Reprinted by permission of Farrar, Straus and Giroux, LLC.

Tennyson, Alfred Lord, 1809–1917
   The Song of the Brook
   Poetry of the Victorian Period by Jerome Hamilton Buckley &
   George Benjamin Woods, Scott, Foresman & Co, USA, 1965.

Thomas, Edward, 1878–1917
   The Brook
   The Mill-Water
   The Watchers
   Collected Poems, Faber & Faber, 1979.
   Reproduced by permission of Myfanwy Thomas.

Thomas, R. S., 1913–
   The River
   Later Poems 1972–1982, Macmillan, 1984. © R. S. Thomas,
   1984. Reproduced by permission of Macmillan Publishers Ltd
   and the author.

Thompson, James, 1700–1748
   'Wide o'er the Brim, with many a Torrent swell'd'
   The Seasons, edited by James Sambrook, Oxford University
   Press, 1981.

Thwaite, Anthony, 1930–
   At Dunkeswell Abbey
   Poems 1953–1988, Hutchinson, 1989. © Anthony Thwaite
   1989. Reproduced by permission of the author.

Tomlinson, Charles, 1927–
   Hudson River School
   Ruskin Remembered
   Annunciations, Oxford University Press, 1989.

   Severnside
   Collected Poems, Oxford University Press, 1985. © Charles
   Tomlinson 1985/1989. Reproduced by permission of the author
   and Oxford University Press.

Vince, Michael, 1947–
   Riverside
   The Orchard Well, Carcanet Press, 1978. © Michael Vince
   1978. Reproduced by permission of Carcanet Press.

Ward, John Powell, 1937–
    The Wye Below Bredwardine
    Genesis, Seren Books, 1996. © John Powell Ward 1996.
    Reproduced by permission of the author.

Wells, Robert, 1947–
    The Stream
    Lusus, Carcanet Press, 1999. © Robert Wells 1999.
    Reproduced by permission of Carcanet Press.

Whitman, Walt, 1819–1892
    Two Rivulets
    The Voice of the Rain
    The Complete Poems, edited by Francis Murphy, Penguin
    Books, 1975.

Wilde, Oscar, 1854–1900
    Symphony in Yellow
    Poems on the Underground, new and extended edition, edited
    by Gerard Benson, Judith Chernaik and Cicely Herbert, Cassell
    Publishers Ltd, 1994. Reproduced by permission of The Orion
    Publishing Group Ltd.

Williams, William Carlos 1883–1963
    A Flowing River
    Mists over the River
    The Collected Poems 1939–1962, Carcanet Press, 1988.
    Reproduced by permission of Carcanet Press.

Wingfield, Sheila, 1906–1992
    Sonnet
    Collected Poems 1938–1983, Enitharmon Press, 1983.
    Reproduced by permission of Enitharmon Press.

Wolcot, John
    Ballade to a Fish of the Brooke
    Voices: An Anthology of Poetry and Pictures, the second book,
    edited by Geoffrey Summerfield, Penguin Education, 1968.

Wordsworth, William, 1770–1850
    Bathing
    Composed upon Westminster Bridge
    Derwent River
    Selections from Wordsworth, Ginn & Co Ltd, 1932/1958.

Wright, David, 1920–
    On the River Avon, near Stratford
    Poems & Versions, Carcanet Press, 1992. © David Wright
    1992. Reproduced by permission of Carcanet Press.

About Common Ground

Common Ground offers ideas, information and inspiration to help people to learn about, enjoy and take more responsibility for their own localities.

In the spectrum of environmental organisations, Common Ground uniquely pioneers imaginative work on nature, culture and place. We link people, landscape, wild life, buildings, history and customs, as well as bridging philosophy and practice, environment and the arts.

We explore new ways of looking at the world to excite people into remembering the richness of everyday landscapes, common wild life and ordinary places, to savour the symbolisms with which we have endowed nature, to revalue our emotional engagement with places and all that they mean to us, and go to on to become involved in their care.

In raising awareness and action through model projects, exhibitions, publications and events, we are attempting to create a popular culture of wanting to care: we believe that the only way in which we shall achieve a sustainable relationship with nature is by everyone taking part in the effort. 'Holding Your Ground: an action guide to local conservation' in 1985 established our role in informing local environmental action and cultural expression.

In reasserting the importance of liberating .our subjective response to the world about us, we often work with people for whom this is everyday currency—poets, sculptors, composers, painters, writers, performers—people from all branches of the arts.

Our projects include the campaign for Local Distinctiveness; Save our Orchards; Apple Day; Parish Maps; Local Flora Britannica; Rhynes, Rivers & Running Brooks; and Confluence, which is helping people to create new music for the River Stour in Somerset, Wiltshire and Dorset.

Common Ground is a charity (NO. 326335), formed in 1983. We seek no members and create no structures. Through collaborations we build links between organisations and disciplines, local people and professionals. We act as a catalyst and mentor; by broadcasting ideas and demonstrating by example we try to extend the constituencies for conservation and create foundations for real democracy.

Publications by Common Ground

FIELD DAYS: *An Anthology of Poetry*, edited by Angela King and Susan Clifford for Common Ground with a foreword by Adam Nicolson, Green Books, 1998. See opposite page for details. £8.95 + £1.05 p&p.

A MANIFESTO FOR FIELDS makes 41 arguments for fairer fields. A5, 24 pages with illustrations by leading artists. 1997. £3.50 + 50p p&p.

FIELD DAYS: *Ideas for Investigations and Celebrations* is packed with a wide range of suggestions and examples to encourage Field Day activities, from surveys to picnics, promoting a greater awareness of the importance of fields and active local participation in their future. A5, 24 pages with illustrations by leading artists. 1997. £3.50 + 50p p&p.

LOCAL DISTINCTIVENESS: *Place, Particularity and Identity, essays for a conference* including papers by Neal Ascherson, Edward Chorlton, Gillian Darley, Roger Deakin, Michael Dower, Richard Mabey and Patrick Wright. 1993. £5.95 + £1.50 p&p.

CELEBRATING LOCAL DISTINCTIVENESS: *Common Ground for Rural Action* gives examples of how people are reinforcing local identity. Provides anyone with an interest in environmental action and the arts in rural areas with a fascinating gathering of examples that are both persuasive and practical. 1994. £3.00 + 50p p&p.

FROM PLACE TO PLACE: *Maps and Parish Maps*. Writings about maps and places. Sets the scene for an idea which challenges communities to explore, express and care for the things they value in their everyday places. Writers including Barbara Bender, Robin Grove-White, Simon Lewty, Richard Mabey and Adam Nicolson are joined by people describing their experiences of Parish Mapping. 1996. £10.00 + £1.50 p&p.

TREES BE COMPANY: *An Anthology of Poetry*, edited by Angela King and Susan Clifford with a foreword by John Fowles. First published by Bristol Classical Press in 1989, this anthology reveals the vital influence of trees and woods on our literature and on our ways of seeing the world. Publication by Green Books (Chelsea Green in the USA) is planned for Autumn 2000. See page 224 for details.

For most recent information, please see our web site:
<www.commonground.org.uk> or send s.a.e. to:

Common Ground, P.O. BOX 25309, London NW5 1ZA, UK.

Also available—a companion volume:

FIELD DAYS

An Anthology of Poetry

Edited by Angela King and Susan Clifford for

Common Ground

With a Foreword by Adam Nicolson

Fields and meadows lie near the heart of our understanding of nature. Yet they are under increasing attack: from development, from intensive agriculture, including agrochemicals, and now from genetic engineering. Their essential qualities, and changing character through time and the seasons, have been celebrated over the centuries by poets, who illuminate the real partnership between humankind and nature that fields—the unwritten history of our relationship with the land—represent.

This anthology brings together the work of more than ninety poets, ancient and modern, including Wendell Berry, John Betjeman, John Burnside, Helen Dunmore, Ivor Gurney, Seamus Heaney, Elizabeth Jennings, John Keats, Alice Oswald, Kathleen Raine and Walt Whitman.

UK edition published by Green Books
ISBN 1 870098 73 0 £8.95

USA edition published by Chelsea Green
ISBN 1 890132 25 X $14.95

*In Autumn 2000 we shall publish
the third and final volume in this series:*

TREES BE
COMPANY

An Anthology of Poetry

Edited by Angela King and Susan Clifford for

Common Ground

This anthology takes the presence of trees and woodland as its central theme. Many poets—particularly twentieth-century writers—are represented, and the collection reveals the vital influence on literature and our ways of seeing the world that tree-and-woodland images continue to exert, despite the widespread neglect and abuse of our natural environment.

John Fowles writes in his Foreword: 'We are all heir to two conflicting souls, or psyches, when it comes to nature: a green one and a black. The first, best symbolized by the tree, still retains at least a memory of what it was to live in balance of a kind with nature, on a green planet.'

(*Trees be Company* was first published as an individual volume
by Bristol Classical Press in 1989.)